500

cupcakes
& muffins

500

cupcakes

& muffins

fergal connolly

APPLE

A Quintet Book

Published by Apple Press in 2006
7 Greenland Street
London NW1 0ND
United Kingdom

www.apple-press.com

ISBN: 978-1-84543-095-5
QUIN. LCUP

Reprinted 2006, 2007 (twice), 2008, 2009 (twice)

This book was designed and produced by
Quintet Publishing Limited
6 Blundell Street
London N7 9BH

Project Editor: Jenny Doubt
Associate Project Editor: Rebecca Warren
Editor: Marianne Canty
Art Director: Roland Codd
Photography: Ian Garlick
Home Economist: Fergal Connolly
Publisher: Judith More
Managing Editor: Jane Laing

Manufactured in Singapore by Pica Digital Pte Ltd.
Printed in China by SNP Leefung Printers Ltd.

contents

introduction

Whether it's their individual size, their pretty icing, or just their ability to bring back fond memories of childhood, cupcakes really do have ultimate treat-appeal. Every generation seems to love them, and even the most curmudgeonly among us will find it hard to fight off a smile when presented with a plateful of cupcakes.

Cupcakes come in many shapes and guises, but the one thing they all have in common is that they're small, individual-sized cakes baked in a muffin tin or cup-shaped moulds, which are often lined with pleated foil or paper baking cases. You can make cupcakes by baking almost any cake batter in a cup-shaped mould. Classic yellow cake or pound cake mixtures are particularly popular, but gingerbread, carrot cakes, fruit cakes, yeasted cakes and brownies can all be transformed into cupcakes. They may be iced, decorated, glazed, dusted with icing sugar, or left unadorned – and whichever you choose, they're sure to be delicious.

As well as making traditional baked cupcakes, you can steam some mixtures to make dense, moist desserts, like bread pudding. You can make other cupcakes using the no-bake method, in which you spoon a mixture of melted and dry ingredients into cupcake moulds and chill or leave them until set. These unbaked cupcakes are usually served without icing, or simply dusted with a little icing sugar or unsweetened cocoa powder.

types of cupcakes

Cupcakes go by many different names. Some describe specific types of cakes, while others are more generic. Muffins, a huge category of cupcakes, are leavened with baking powder (and occasionally yeast) and are often baked without paper baking cases. Sweet or savoury, they can be eaten as a breakfast treat, with afternoon tea, or as an accompaniment to lunch or dinner. Muffins are not usually iced, although they may have a topping added before baking – for example, a sprinkling of coarse sugar, a streusal topping or grated Parmesan cheese.

Madeleines are a classic French cupcake baked in a shell-shaped mould. They are made with a mixture of egg yolks beaten with sugar and lemon zest, then combined with flour, hazelnut butter, and whisked egg whites. They are usually served plain, without icing.

Spain has its own traditional cupcakes. *Sobaos pasiegas* are rich sponge cakes baked in individual rectangular papers, while simple *magdalenas* resemble a more classic round cupcake. Rich and buttery, both are eaten without plain.

Queen cakes are a traditional British cupcake made with a creamed butter mixture combined with currants, lemon zest and sometimes chopped almonds. Traditionally, they were baked in small, fluted moulds, but today they are more usually baked in pleated paper baking cases or muffin tins.

Even in Southeast Asia you'll find little cupcakes. In the Philippines, mooncakes – rice cakes steamed in banana leaf cups – are a delicious treat. In Japan, small sponge cakes known as *katsutera* are popular.

icing cupcakes
Although some cupcakes are served plain, it is the icing that makes many cupcakes. Whether it's a thick smear of cream cheese icing or an intricately decorated cake topped with fondant decorations, it's the topping that often causes the greatest delight, not just for the sweet, luscious flavour it adds to a simple cake. Children and adults alike will love helping decorate the cupcakes, and it can make a fun afternoon activity before you even get around to sitting down with a glass of milk to enjoy them. Once you get started on the recipes in this book, you'll realise just how fun baking and decorating cupcakes can be, and you might just find yourself with a whole new hobby!

equipment

Most cupcakes and muffins are incredibly simple to make, and you'll only need a few pieces of equipment.

scales, measuring jugs, cups & spoons
Accurate weighing scales and/or calibrated measuring jugs, as well as proper measuring spoons, are essential for successful baking. If the proportions of ingredients are incorrect, the cupcake or muffin may not rise and/or set properly.

mixing bowls & spoons
You will need a medium bowl and wooden spoon for mixing most cupcake batters. Smaller bowls are useful for for mixing small quantities. A large metal spoon is useful for folding ingredients into delicate whisked mixtures. Unless otherwise stipulated, use a medium bowl for the recipes in this book.

sieves
You will need a large sieve for sieving dry ingredients such as flour and a small one for dusting icing sugar or cocoa over baked cupcakes.

muffin tins
Muffin tins are the most user-friendly tins for making standard cupcakes. The standard muffin tin has 6 or 12 cup-shaped indentations. You can line them with paper baking cases, or simply grease them before filling them with batter. The standard muffin cup is approximately 6 cm (2½ in) in diameter. If you are not filling all of the cups with batter, simply fill the otherwise empty cups with water prior to baking.

other cupcake moulds

You can bake cupcakes in other moulded tins. Shell-shaped madeleine tins are widely available. You may also find other tins with decorative, ridged cups in a variety of sizes. Individual stainless steel moulds or cups can also be used to bake cupcakes.

baking cases

Pleated paper or foil baking cases are available in many sizes, from tiny petit four cups for making miniature cupcakes and muffins, to giant baking cups for extra-big and colourful breakfast treats.

timers

Perfect timing is essential for success, so always use a timer when baking. Accurate digital timers are inexpensive and well worth the investment.

wire racks

Cupcakes should usually be left in the tin to cool for 5 minutes, before they are transferred to a wire rack to cool completely. Wire racks come in a variety of shapes and sizes.

other equipment

An electric whisk can be a useful time saver, and is great when making all-in-one cupcake mixtures. The whisk should be set on medium speed unless otherwise indicated. A sharp, serrated knife with a pointed end can help slice the tops off cupcakes, or make a hollow in which to spoon filling.

ingredients

Most cupcake mixtures have four basic ingredients: fat, sugar, eggs and flour. Other ingredients, such as chocolate, nuts and dried fruit, are frequently added.

butter & other fats

Unsalted butter is usually best for cupcake mixtures; it gives a wonderfully rich flavour. For creamed cupcake mixtures, use butter at room temperature; for rubbed-in mixtures, use cold, firm butter; and for melted mixtures, dice the butter before gently warming it. Margarine, white cooking fats, and mild-tasting vegetable oils sometimes replace butter and are a good choice for those with a dairy intolerance or allergy. Butter and cream cheese should always be softened before adding to the recipe unless otherwise stated.

sugar & other sweeteners

There are many different types of sugar, all of which add their own unique taste and texture to cupcake mixtures. Refined white sugars add sweetness, while brown sugars add flavour and colour as well. The texture of the sugar will also affect the cupcake. Caster sugar is most frequently used for cupcakes, but coarser-textured sugars such as raw sugar, and moist sugars such as brown sugar, are also used. Icing sugar is generally used for dusting cupcakes and making icing.

Golden syrup, maple syrup, honey and treacle can also be used in cupcakes, either in place of, or alongside, sugar. They give a distinctive taste and texture, and are a frequent addition to melted cupcake mixtures.

flour & flour alternatives

Most cupcake mixtures call for self-raising flour or plain flour, with the addition of a leavening agent. Wholemeal flour is sometimes used, but it produces cupcakes with a heavier, denser texture. Non-wheat flours, often combined with wheat flour, may also be used. These include polenta, oatmeal, cornflour and rice flour. Ground nuts may be used in place of flour and are particularly good for gluten-free cupcakes.

eggs
Eggs enrich cupcake mixtures and help to bind ingredients together. For the best results, use eggs at room temperature. When whisking egg whites, be sure to use a clean, grease-free bowl. Eggs should always be lightly beaten before adding to the recipe unless otherwise stated.

other ingredients & flavourings
Dried fruits, nuts and seeds are a popular addition to cupcake mixtures. Dried fruits add natural sweetness, so you may be able to use less sugar than in a plain cupcake mixture. Different dried fruits are often interchangeable in recipes.

Fresh fruit such as mashed bananas, apples, pineapples and berries may also be folded into cupcake batters. Frozen fruit may be substituted for the recipes in this book. Thoroughly thaw and drain before adding to the recipe.

Chocolate, another popular ingredient, may be used to flavour or bind cake mixtures or to decorate baked cupcakes. For the recipes in this book, you'll need unsweetened cocoa powder, chocolate chips or chunks, and different varieties of baking chocolate in your pantry.

Vanilla-flavoured pie filling may be substituted for custard.

Always assume that herbs used in the recipes are dried, unless fresh is specified.

Other ingredients and flavourings include marshmallows, spices, herbs, cheese, vanilla, coffee, citrus zest, almond essence, orange flower water, rosewater and liqueurs.

making cupcakes

There are four main types of cupcake mixtures. The order in which ingredients are added, and the way they are combined – for example, beaten or folded in – will affect the final texture of the cupcakes.

preparing the tin

When the recipe calls for the tin to be greased, you may use any fat you choose. Smear a little butter, margarine, or olive oil on a paper towel and wipe each cup thoroughly. Low-calorie sprays can also be used for this purpose.

creamed mixtures

For creamed mixtures, you begin by creaming the sugar and fat together to make a light, fluffy mixture before beating in eggs. Self-raising flour (or plain flour and a leavening agent such as baking powder) is then folded in, along with any other flavouring ingredients. The mixture should then be poured into baking cases and baked immediately. Moisture and heat cause tiny bubbles of carbon dioxide to be released, producing cupcakes with a light and fluffy texture.

Sometimes baking powder may be replaced with bicarbonate of soda and an acidic ingredient, such as vinegar, cider or buttermilk. These substitutes all work effectively to help the cupcake rise while it is baking.

all-in-one mixtures

This technique is literally "all in one": put all the ingredients in a bowl and beat them until smooth. Fold in additional ingredients such as dried fruit, then pour the batter into the tin(s) for baking.

whisked mixtures

The classic cupcake mixture is whisked. Begin by whisking eggs and sugar. Then fold in the flour and other dry ingredients. The air bubbles expand in the heat, causing the cupcake to rise and giving it a spongy texture.

muffin mixtures

For muffins, you usually combine the dry ingredients in one bowl, and the melted fat and any liquid ingredients in another. Pour the liquid ingredients into the dry ingredients and stir until just combined. Overmixing will give tough, chewy results, rather than light, fluffy muffins – so don't worry if there are still a few streaks of flour in the batter as you spoon it into the cups.

general baking tips

When adding batter to a tin, you may either spoon or pour the batter into the baking cases. Each case should be two-thirds full unless otherwise stated. If the tin has empty cups, fill these halfway with water to ensure even baking. Use caution when removing the tin from the oven, the water will be hot. When baking, the tins should be placed in the centre of the oven. As oven temperatures vary by model, cupcakes should be tested for doneness a few minutes before advised baking time. If a skewer inserted into the centre of the cake comes out clean, it is done.

storing

Cupcakes made with a high proportion of fat can be stored in an airtight container for several days. Muffins and low-fat cupcakes are usually best eaten on the day of making. For the best results, store cakes without icing, and decorate on the day of serving. Cupcakes usually freeze well and can be frozen, without icing, in an airtight container for up to 3 months.

decorating cupcakes

Golden muffins look fabulous as they are – risen and craggy with their puffed-up tops – but cupcakes are the treats that you can really go to town on when it comes to decoration. A simple spoonful of icing with a cherry on top or a drizzle of melted chocolate is just the start. Supermarkets and specialist cookery shops sell a host of ingredients and equipment to help you – from food colouring and ready-made icing to edible sugared flowers and brightly coloured sweets. Here are a few ideas that will help you transform the simplest cupcakes into a stunning centrepiece for a party or dessert.

getting started
If you're going for simply iced cupcakes – perhaps with a dollop of frosting and a big coloured sweet or whole nut on top – leave the cupcake as it is, with its risen domed top. However, if you want to go for a more intricately decorated cupcake – perhaps with a pattern iced on top, or lots of sweets – slice off the top of the cupcake to give you a flat surface. Always wait for cupcakes to cool before icing them.

decorating unbaked cupcakes
Unbaked cupcakes and muffins can be sprinkled with coarse sugar, whole, chopped, or flaked nuts or dried fruit, or a piece of fresh fruit such as a slice of apple or peach. Don't top them with anything too heavy or it may sink into the batter during baking. Finely grated Parmesan cheese can make a good topping for savoury muffins.

dusting and sprinkling
The simplest way to decorate freshly baked cupcakes is to dust them with icing sugar or unsweetened cocoa.

fondant icing
Perfect for rolling out and draping over cupcakes, this firm icing can also be coloured and made into decorations to attach to cakes. You can make it yourself, but it's so much easier to buy ready-to-roll fondant icing and simply colour it yourself. To make it yourself, simply add a few drops of food colouring and then thoroughly knead the fondant. Repeat until the desired colour is achieved.

coloured sprinkles, balls & cake decorations
Coloured sprinkles, balls and other cake decorations look great on cupcakes. Look in specialist cookery shops for frosted flowers, pastel-coloured sugared almonds, and other pretty, edible decorations. First top the cupcakes with icing or melted chocolate, then allow it to set slightly before pressing on the decorations. If you prefer a cupcake without too much icing, use only a small blob to attach individual sweets or decorations – they'll look just as pretty but won't be nearly so sweet.

fresh fruit
Pretty summer berries look delightful (and taste delectable) on top of iced cupcakes. They're particularly good on cupcakes topped with buttercream or cream cheese icing. Or even simpler, just spoon a big dollop of whipped cream on top of each cupcake and top with a few fresh raspberries or strawberries.

simple fillings
The simplest filling is flavoured whipped cream. Try sweetening whipped cream with a little icing sugar and adding a few drops of vanilla or peppermint essence, rosewater, or citrus zest. Honey and maple syrup make good flavourings, as do liqueurs such as cointreau.

serving & cupcake gifts

Cupcakes are often associated with children, but offer a plate of cupcakes to fully grown adults and you're sure to see their faces light up. Whether it's a rack of warm, wholesome muffins or a glittering cake stand piled high with pretty, pastel-coloured confections – cupcakes are always a hit and seem to appeal to every generation.

cakes on the move
Baked in their own wrappers, these lovely cakes aren't just for eating at home. An individual, portion-sized cake is great for eating on the move – whether it's a breakfast muffin to eat on the run, a treat to go in a lunchbox, an energy-boosting snack to take on a long walk, or an easy dessert to serve at a picnic.

dashing desserts
There's something wonderfully informal yet utterly appealing about cupcakes that makes them a great alternative to dessert after a special meal. Who's got time to make a dessert after an appetiser and main course – and who's really got room to fit one in? Why not bring out a plate of prettily decorated cupcakes with coffee instead? You're sure to get just as much praise as you would for a dessert that takes hours to make.

celebrating with cupcakes
Big celebration cakes are a thing of the past. What everyone wants now is a towering pile of cupcakes. For birthdays, pile up cupcakes on a plate and stick them with birthday candles and baby indoor sparklers to really get the celebrations going. This alternative to the traditional cake is particularly good for kids' parties, where little children can struggle with a big slice of cake – or for adult parties where everyone's trying to watch their waistlines!

Huge tiered wedding cakes are off the agenda for those in the know. For a real impact at your wedding, go for pretty white wedding cupcakes piled high on a cake stand, or arranged in tiers. It makes serving so much easier – and guests will love them.

Spoil your loved one with love heart cupcakes on Valentine's Day, or scare them at Halloween with a plate of spooky cakes. On Independence Day, join in the celebrations with a tray of stars-and-stripes cupcakes, and on St. Patrick's Day, start the festivities at breakfast time with a special St. Patrick's Day muffin.

special gifts

Cupcakes make great gifts, and you're sure to put a smile on the face of the recipient. They're usually best packed in a single layer, with a little tissue paper tucked around them to make sure they don't move around as you transport them. Pretty boxes with clear plastic lids are a good choice, particularly for cupcakes with decorative icing. They're available from stationery and department stores, so look around and see what you can find.

Flat baskets make another pretty way to deliver your cupcakes. Arrive at a brunch party with a basket full of warm muffins and your host – and the other guests – will love you for them!

Cupcakes with a firm icing (such as fondant or royal icing) can look pretty wrapped up individually in clear cellophane. Cut out a large square of cellophane, place a cupcake in the centre, then pull up the edges around the cake and tie with ribbon. These individually wrapped cakes make great going-home presents after a kids' party or festive wedding favours.

You can also decorate the foil or paper baking cases that contain the cupcakes. Try tying pretty ribbon around each cake, or cut out a round of pretty fabric, place the cupcake in the centre, and tie up firmly with coordinating ribbon.

classic cupcakes

These cupcakes have delighted generations. From the classic combination of apple and cinnamon to the irresistibly rich pairing of rum and raisin, all the best-loved recipes are here.

spanish orange syrup cupcakes

see variations page 42

Make these sticky cupcakes ahead of time to let the syrup soak through.

for the cupcakes
2 medium seedless sweet oranges, peeled
   and roughly chopped
115 g (4 oz) unsalted butter
225 g (8 oz) caster sugar
2 eggs
60 g (2½ oz) semolina

60 g (2½ oz) ground almonds
60 g (2½ oz) self-raising flour

for the syrup
1 peeled orange rind, from cupcake recipe
100 g (3½ oz) caster sugar
225 ml (8 fl oz) water

Preheat the oven to 160°C (325°F / Gas mark 3). Place 12 paper baking cases in a muffin tin.
In a saucepan, cover the oranges with water. Simmer until tender, about 15 minutes. Cool.
Drain the oranges and purée in a food processor. In a bowl, beat the butter and sugar with
an electric whisk until light. Slowly beat in the eggs. Stir in the rest of the ingredients, along
with the orange purée, until well combined. Spoon the mixture into the cases. Bake for
35 minutes. Remove pan from the oven and cool.

To make the syrup, thinly slice the orange rind, removing the pith. Cut the orange rind into
thin strips. In a pan, bring the sugar and water to a simmer, stirring to dissolve the sugar.
Add the orange strips and boil uncovered for 5 minutes, or until tender. Spoon the syrup
onto each cupcake. Store in an airtight container for up to 2 days.

Makes 1 dozen

vanilla cupcakes

see variations page 43

The grand dame of cupcakes. If you can get vanilla sugar, use half caster and half vanilla caster. This will really enhance the vanilla flavour.

225 g (8 oz) unsalted butter, softened
225 g (8 oz) caster sugar
225 g (8 oz) self-raising flour

1 tsp baking powder
4 eggs
1 tsp vanilla essence

Preheat the oven to 175°C (350°F / Gas mark 4). Place 18 paper baking cases in muffin tins.

Place all the ingredients in a medium bowl and beat with an electric whisk until smooth and pale, about 2 to 3 minutes.

Spoon the mixture into the cases. Bake for 20 minutes.

Remove the tins from the oven and cool for 5 minutes. Then remove the cupcakes and cool on a rack.

Store in an airtight container for up to 3 days, or freeze for up to 3 months.

Makes 1¹/₂ dozen

gingerbread pots

see variations page 44

You could make these dense, sticky gingerbread cupcakes in terra cotta pots to give them a rustic charm. The sharp lemon drizzle helps to cut the sweetness of the gingerbread.

for the gingerbread
150 g (5 oz) self-raising flour
150 g (5 oz) wholemeal self-raising flour
1 tbsp baking powder
4 tsp ground ginger
1 tsp cinnamon
225 g (8 oz) light brown sugar
2 eggs

115 ml (4 fl oz) honey
115 g (4 oz) unsalted butter, melted
175 ml (6 fl oz) milk
2 tbsp roughly chopped crystallised ginger

for the drizzle
125 g (4½ oz) icing sugar
5 tbsp lemon juice

Preheat the oven to 175°C (350°F / Gas mark 4). Place 12 paper baking cases in a muffin tin or line 12 small terra cotta pots with greaseproof paper. Sieve the flours, baking powder, ginger and cinnamon into a large bowl. In a medium bowl combine the remaining ingredients and beat with an electric whisk until smooth, about 2 to 3 minutes. Stir into the dry ingredients. Spoon the batter into the cases.

Bake for 20 minutes. Remove tin or pots from the oven and cool for 10 minutes. Then remove cupcakes and cool on a rack. To make the drizzle, sieve the icing sugar into a bowl and slowly add the lemon juice, stirring until just combined. Drizzle over the tops of the cupcakes. Store in an airtight container for up to 3 days.

Makes 1 dozen

lemon butterfly cupcakes

see variations page 45

You'll love these delicate little numbers, which can be served with tea or as a dessert.

for the cupcakes
225 g (8 oz) unsalted butter, softened
225 g (8 oz) caster sugar
225 g (8 oz) self-raising flour
1 tsp baking powder
4 eggs
1 tsp vanilla essence

for the icing
115 g (4 oz) unsalted butter
225 g (8 oz) icing sugar, sieved
1 tsp vanilla essence
1 tbsp lemon zest

Preheat the oven to 175°C (350°F / Gas mark 4). Place 18 paper baking cases in muffin tins. Combine all ingredients for the cupcakes in a large bowl and beat with an electric whisk until smooth and pale, about 2 to 3 minutes. Spoon the batter into the cases.

Bake for 20 minutes. Remove tins from the oven and cool for 5 minutes. Then remove the cupcakes and cool on a rack.

Prepare the icing by beating the butter, icing sugar, vanilla and lemon zest until smooth. Cut a slice from the top of each cake and cut it into two. Pipe the icing onto the flattened top of each cupcake. Then place the half-circles of cake at an angle on each side of the icing.

Store without icing in an airtight container for up to 3 days, or freeze for up to 3 months.

Makes 1¹/₂ dozen

rum & raisin cupcakes

see variations page 46

Use dark rum in this recipe to give these cupcakes a warm Caribbean feel.

for the cupcakes
75 g (3 oz) raisins
3 tbsp dark rum
225 g (8 oz) unsalted butter, softened
225 g (8 oz) caster sugar
225 g (8 oz) self-raising flour

1 tsp baking powder
4 eggs

for the syrup
5 tbsp dark rum
2 tbsp light brown sugar

Soak the raisins in the rum for 2 to 3 hours or overnight to soften them. Drain. Preheat the oven to 175°C (350°F / Gas mark 4). Place 18 paper baking cases in muffin tins. Combine all the cupcake ingredients in a large bowl and beat with an electric whisk until smooth and pale, about 2 to 3 minutes. Stir in the sultanas. Spoon the batter into the cases. Bake for 20 minutes.

While the cupcakes are in the oven, combine the syrup ingredients in a pan. Over low heat, dissolve the sugar in the rum. Simmer for 5 minutes, then remove from the heat. Remove tins from the oven. With a toothpick, prick 5 holes in each cupcake and pour the warm syrup over them. Then remove the cupcakes and cool on a rack.

Store in an airtight container for up to 3 days, or freeze for up to 3 months.

Makes 1¹/₂ dozen

mini raspberry & coconut cupcakes

see variations page 47

The inspiration for these cupcakes came from the classic English Bakewell tart.

3 tbsp ground almonds
40 g (1½ oz) desiccated coconut
175 g (6 oz) icing sugar, sieved
200 g (7 oz) plain flour
1 tsp baking powder

115 g (4 oz) unsalted butter, melted
5 egg whites
115 g (4 oz) fresh or thawed, frozen raspberries
2 tbsp desiccated coconut, to finish

Preheat the oven to 190°C (375°F / Gas mark 5). Place 24 mini ceramic baking cases on a baking tray.

In a large bowl, combine the ground almonds, coconut, icing sugar, flour and baking powder. Stir in the butter, followed by the egg whites.

Spoon the mixture into the cases. Drop a raspberry and a little desiccated coconut on top of each cupcake. Bake for 12 to 15 minutes. Remove the cases from the oven and cool for 5 minutes. Then remove the cupcakes and cool on a rack.

Store in an airtight container for up to 2 days, or freeze in a sealed container for up to 3 months.

Makes 2 dozen

carrot & walnut cupcakes

see variations page 48

Carrot cake somehow doesn't seem to be as naughty as other cakes!

for the cupcakes
225 g (8 oz) unsalted butter, softened
225 g (8 oz) caster sugar
225 g (8 oz) self-raising flour
4 eggs
1 tsp mixed spice
100 g (3½ oz) chopped walnuts
150 g (5 oz) freshly grated carrots
2 tbsp sultanas

for the icing
200 g (7 oz) cream cheese, softened
175 g (6 oz) icing sugar, sieved
1 tbsp lemon juice
1 tsp vanilla essence
3 tbsp chopped walnuts

Preheat the oven to 175°C (350°F / Gas mark 4). Place 18 baking cases in muffin tins. Combine the butter, sugar, flour and eggs in a large bowl and beat with an electric whisk until smooth, about 2 to 3 minutes. Stir in the rest of the ingredients. Spoon the batter into the cases. Bake for 20 minutes. Remove tins from the oven and cool for 5 minutes. Then remove the cupcakes and cool on a rack. To make the icing, slowly beat the cream cheese and icing sugar in a large bowl with an electric whisk until creamy and soft. Add the lemon juice and vanilla and beat briskly until well combined. Spread the icing liberally onto the cooled cupcakes and garnish with the chopped walnuts.

Store without icing for up to 3 days in an airtight container, or freeze for up to 3 months.

Makes about 1½ dozen

very cherry cupcakes

see variations page 49

Maraschino cherries give these cupcakes a wonderful rich flavour.

for the cupcakes
225 g (8 oz) unsalted butter, softened
225 g (8 oz) caster sugar
225 g (8 oz) self-raising flour
1 tsp baking powder
4 eggs
2 tbsp kirsch

for the icing
375 g (13 oz) icing sugar, sieved
225 g (8 oz) unsalted butter
Pinch of salt
Red food colouring
12 bottled morello or maraschino cherries
    with stems

Preheat the oven to 175°C (350°F / Gas mark 4). Place 18 paper baking cases in muffin tins.

Combine all the cupcake ingredients in a large bowl and beat with an electric whisk until smooth, about 2 to 3 minutes. Spoon the batter into the cases. Bake for 20 minutes. Remove tins from the oven and cool for 5 minutes. Then remove the cupcakes and cool on a rack. To make the icing, beat the icing sugar, butter and salt in a medium bowl with an electric whisk until smooth. Add a few drops of the food colouring and beat until well combined and pink. Spread the icing onto the cooled cupcakes and garnish with a cherry on top.

Store without icing in an airtight container for up to 3 days, or freeze for up to 3 months.

Makes 1¹/₂ dozen

classic chocolate buttercream cupcakes

see variations page 50

The plain chocolate in this recipe gives the icing a wonderful glossy sheen.

for the cupcakes
225 g (8 oz) unsalted butter, softened
225 g (8 oz) caster sugar
225 g (8 oz) self-raising flour
1 tsp baking powder
4 tbsp Dutch-process cocoa powder
4 eggs
1 tsp vanilla essence

for the icing
100 g (3½ oz) chopped plain chocolate
2 tbsp double cream
50 g (2 oz) unsalted butter, softened
100 g (3½ oz) icing sugar, sieved

Preheat the oven to 175°C (350°F / Gas mark 4). Place 18 paper baking cases in muffin tins. Combine all the cupcake ingredients in a large bowl and beat with an electric whisk until smooth, about 2 to 3 minutes. Spoon the batter into the cases. Bake for 20 minutes. Remove tins from the oven and cool for 5 minutes. Then remove the cupcakes and cool on a rack. For the icing, put the chocolate, cream and butter in a pan over low heat. Stir gently until combined. Remove from the heat and stir in the icing sugar until the mixture is smooth. Swirl onto the cupcakes.

Store without icing in an airtight container for up to 2 days.

Makes 1½ dozen

apple sauce &
cinnamon cupcakes

see variations page 51

Cinnamon brings a delicate sweetness to this cupcake recipe and complements the apple sauce marvellously.

115 g (4 oz) unsalted butter, softened
115 g (4 oz) caster sugar
115 g (4 oz) self-raising flour
2 eggs
115 g (4 oz) unsweetened apple sauce

¾ tsp cinnamon
50 g (2 oz) chopped pecans
75 g (3 oz) sultanas
1 small red eating apple, thinly sliced
2 tbsp granulated sugar

Preheat the oven to 175°C (350°F / Gas mark 4). Grease a 12-cup muffin tin. Place the butter, sugar, flour and egg in a bowl and beat with an electric whisk until smooth, about 2 to 3 minutes. Stir in the apple sauce, cinnamon, pecans and sultanas.

Spoon the batter into the cups. Lay the apple slices on top and sprinkle with a little sugar.

Bake for 25 minutes. Remove tin from the oven and cool for 5 minutes. Then remove the cupcakes and cool on a rack. Serve warm.

Store in an airtight container for up to 3 days, or freeze for up to 3 months.

Makes 1 dozen

peanut butter cupcakes

see variations page 52

The texture of crunchy peanut butter in this recipe is excellent, though creamier varieties also work.

for the cupcakes
225 g (8 oz) unsalted butter, softened
225 g (8 oz) caster sugar
225 g (8 oz) self-raising flour
4 eggs
115 g (4 oz) crunchy peanut butter

for the icing
60 g (2½ oz) crunchy peanut butter
50 g (2 oz) unsalted butter, softened
2 tsp vanilla essence
115 g (4 oz) icing sugar, sieved
2 tbsp milk

Preheat the oven to 175°C (350°F / Gas mark 4). Place 18 paper baking cases in muffin tins. Combine the butter, sugar, flour and eggs in a large bowl and beat with an electric whisk until smooth, about 2 to 3 minutes. Stir in the peanut butter until well combined. Spoon the batter into the cases. Bake for 20 minutes. Remove tins from the oven and cool for 5 minutes. Then remove the cupcakes and cool on a rack.

To make the icing, combine the peanut butter, butter and vanilla in a medium bowl. Using an electric whisk beat until light and fluffy, about 1 to 2 minutes. Add the icing sugar along with the milk, and beat until well combined. Swirl the icing onto the cooled cupcakes.

Store without icing in an airtight container for up to 3 days, or freeze for up to 3 months.

Makes 1¹/₂ dozen

poppy seed cupcakes with lemon drizzle

see variations page 53

The poppy seeds give these cupcakes a wonderful crunch!

for the cupcakes
225 g (8 oz) unsalted butter, softened
225 g (8 oz) caster sugar
225 g (8 oz) self-raising flour
4 eggs
1 tsp vanilla essence
1 tbsp poppy seeds
1 tbsp grated lemon zest

for the drizzle
125 g (4½ oz) icing sugar
4 tbsp lemon juice
2 tbsp poppy seeds

Preheat the oven to 175°C (350°F / Gas mark 4). Place 18 paper baking cases in muffin tins. Combine the butter, sugar, flour and eggs in a large bowl and beat with an electric whisk until smooth, about 2 to 3 minutes. Stir in the vanilla, poppy seeds and lemon zest until well combined. Spoon the batter into the cases. Bake for 20 minutes. Remove tins from the oven and cool for 5 minutes. Then remove the cupcakes and cool on a rack. To make the drizzle, sieve the icing sugar into a bowl and stir in the lemon juice until it resembles the consistency of double cream. Stir in the poppy seeds and drizzle over the cupcakes.

Store in an airtight container for up to 2 days, or freeze for up to 3 months.

Makes 1¹/₂ dozen

banana cupcakes

see variations page 54

The subtle flavour of banana perfectly complements the cream cheese icing.

for the cupcakes
225 g (8 oz) unsalted butter, softened
225 g (8 oz) caster sugar
225 g (8 oz) self-raising flour
4 eggs
¼ tsp nutmeg
225 g (8 oz) mashed ripe bananas

for the icing
200 g (7 oz) cream cheese
175 g (6 oz) icing sugar, sieved
1 tbsp lemon juice
1 tsp vanilla essence
1 banana, thinly sliced

Preheat the oven to 175°C (350°F / Gas mark 4). Place 18 paper baking cases in muffin tins. Combine the butter, sugar, flour, eggs and nutmeg in a large bowl and beat with an electric whisk until smooth, about 2 to 3 minutes. Stir in the mashed bananas until well combined. Spoon the batter into the cases. Bake for 20 minutes. Remove tins from the oven and cool for 5 minutes. Then remove the cupcakes and cool on a rack.

To make the icing, slowly beat the cream cheese in a large bowl with an electric whisk until it is soft and smooth. Add the icing sugar, lemon juice and vanilla. Beat briskly until smooth and well combined. Swirl the icing onto the cooled cupcakes. Garnish each cupcake with a banana slice.

Store without icing in an airtight container for up to 3 days, or freeze for up to 3 months.

Makes 1¹/₂ dozen

madeleines

see variations page 55

These light, shell-shaped cupcakes hail from the town of Commercy in the Lorraine region of France.

for the madeleines
4 eggs
175 g (6 oz) caster sugar
125 g (4½ oz) plain flour
1 tsp baking powder
115 g (4 oz) unsalted butter, melted
    and cooled
1 tbsp grated lemon zest

for the glaze
375 g (13 oz) icing sugar, sieved
225 g (8 oz) unsalted butter, softened
Pinch of salt
1 tbsp grated orange zest
Icing sugar, for dusting

Preheat the oven to 175°C (350°F / Gas mark 4). Grease a tin for 18 small madeleines. In a medium bowl, beat the eggs and sugar until pale and thick. Sieve the flour and baking powder into a separate medium bowl. Slowly add the flour to the egg mixture. Pour in the melted butter and stir in the lemon zest. Refrigerate for 20 minutes. Spoon the batter into the tin, filling each mould about two-thirds full. Bake for 20 minutes. Remove tin from the oven and cool for 10 minutes. Then remove the madeleines and cool on a rack. To make the glaze, beat the icing sugar, butter, salt and orange zest together in a bowl using an electric whisk until smooth and creamy. Smear a little glaze on each madeleine and dust with icing sugar.

Store in an airtight container up to 2 days, or freeze for up to 3 months.

Makes 1½ dozen

variations

spanish orange syrup cupcakes

see base recipe page 19

blood orange syrup cupcakes
Prepare the basic cupcake recipe, substituting blood oranges for the sweet oranges.

orange & lemon syrup cupcakes
Prepare the basic cupcake recipe, adding 2 tablespoons lemon juice to the orange purée. For the syrup, zest 1 medium lemon and add with the orange zest to the water and sugar syrup.

grapefruit & orange syrup cupcakes
Prepare the basic cupcake recipe. Add 2 tablespoons grapefruit juice to the orange purée. For the syrup, zest half a medium grapefruit and add it with the orange zest to the water and sugar syrup.

variations

vanilla cupcakes

see base recipe page 21

saffron cupcakes
Prepare the basic cupcake recipe. Add a pinch of saffron to 2 tablespoons boiling water. Infuse for 5 minutes. After creaming the cupcake ingredients, stir in saffron and water.

almond cupcakes
Prepare the basic cupcake recipe, adding 3 tablespoons ground almond to the mixture and substituting 1 teaspoon almond essence for the vanilla essence.

vanilla & sultana cupcakes
Prepare the basic cupcake recipe. After creaming the cupcake ingredients, stir in 75 g (3 oz) sultanas.

variations

gingerbread pots

see base recipe page 22

fruity pots
Fold 75 g (3 oz) mixed chopped dried apricots, raisins and sultanas to the egg mixture before stirring into the dry ingredients.

rhubarb pots
Add 75 g (3 oz) cooked sweetened rhubarb to the egg mixture before stirring in the dry ingredients.

banana pots
Add one mashed banana to the egg mixture before stirring in the dry ingredients.

variations

lemon butterfly cupcakes

see base recipe page 25

orange & lemon butterfly cupcakes
Prepare the basic cupcake recipe. Add 1½ tablespoons grated orange
zest to the icing mixture.

redcurrant butterfly cupcakes
Prepare the basic cupcake recipe. Lightly crush 40 g (1½ oz) fresh or thawed
frozen redcurrants with a fork and add to the icing mixture.

hazelnut & sultana butterfly cupcakes
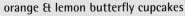
Prepare the basic cupcake recipe. Stir 3 tablespoons roughly chopped
toasted hazelnuts and 2 tablespoons sultanas into the icing mixture
after it has been beaten.

variations

rum & raisin cupcakes

see base recipe page 26

orange liqueur & crystallised peel cupcakes
Prepare the basic cupcake recipe, substituting orange liqueur for the
rum and 75 g (3 oz) chopped crystallised peel for the raisins.

vodka, chilli & chocolate chip cupcakes
Prepare the basic cupcake recipe. Substitute vodka for the rum. Add
1 tablespoon seeded and finely chopped chillies and 75 g (3 oz) plain
chocolate chips in place of the raisins.

malibu & pineapple cupcakes
Prepare the basic cupcake recipe, substituting Malibu for the rum and
75 g (3 oz) finely chopped dried pineapple for the raisins.

variations

mini raspberry & coconut cupcakes

see base recipe page 29

mini blueberry & coconut cupcakes
Prepare the basic cupcake recipe, substituting blueberries for the
raspberries. Add 1 tablespoon finely grated lime zest.

mini blackberry & coconut cupcakes
Prepare the basic cupcake recipe, substituting 50 g (2 oz) blackberries
for the raspberries.

mini lime, mango & coconut cupcakes
Prepare the basic cupcake recipe, substituting 50 g (2 oz) finely
chopped fresh or frozen mango and 1 tablespoon finely grated
lime zest for the raspberries.

variations

carrot & walnut cupcakes

see base recipe page 30

coffee & walnut-iced carrot cupcakes

Prepare the basic cupcake recipe. Add 1 teaspoon hot coffee,
1 teaspoon instant coffee granules and 1 teaspoon coffee liqueur to
the icing mixture. Swirl the coffee icing on top of the cupcakes, and
garnish with chopped walnuts.

orange cream cheese-iced carrot cupcakes

Prepare the basic cupcake recipe. To make the icing, substitute
1 tablespoon orange juice for the lemon juice. Swirl the icing
and garnish with chopped walnuts and finely grated lemon zest.

mascarpone-iced carrot cupcakes

Prepare the basic cupcake recipe. To make the icing, substitute
225 g (8 oz) mascarpone for the cream cheese.

variations

very cherry cupcakes

see base recipe page 31

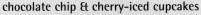

chocolate chip & cherry-iced cupcakes
Prepare the basic cupcake recipe. Stir 100 g (3½ oz) plain chocolate chips into the icing mixture after adding the food colouring.

almond & cherry-iced cupcakes
Prepare the basic cupcake recipe, adding 3 tablespoons ground almonds to the batter mixture. Sprinkle 2 tablespoons of toasted almonds on top of the iced cupcakes, and garnish each with a cherry.

crispy meringue & cherry-iced cupcakes
Prepare the basic cupcake recipe. Place 4 small meringue shells in a plastic food storage bag and lightly crush them with a rolling pin. Gently stir into the icing mixture after adding the food colouring. Swirl onto the cupcakes.

variations

classic chocolate buttercream cupcakes

see base recipe page 32

white & dark choc buttercream cupcakes
Prepare the basic cupcake recipe, stirring 3 tablespoons mixed plain chocolate
chips and white chocolate chips into the creamed batter.

macadamia nut-iced buttercream cupcakes
Prepare the basic cupcake recipe. Lightly toast 60 g (2½ oz) macadamia nuts
and chop finely. Stir the macadamia nuts into the icing mixture after adding
the sugar.

orange & dark choc buttercream cupcakes
Prepare the basic cupcake recipe, substituting 1 tablespoon orange zest for
the vanilla essence.

variations

apple sauce & cinnamon cupcakes

see base recipe page 35

apple sauce & pear cupcakes
Prepare the basic cupcake recipe. Substitute 1 ripe and firm medium-sized
pear for the apple. Lay slices on top of each cupcake and sprinkle with sugar.

apple sauce & warm caramel cupcakes
Prepare the basic cupcake recipe. To make a caramel topping, place 200 g
(7 oz) caramels in a medium pan with 3 tablespoons evaporated milk. Heat
gently, stirring until all the caramels have melted. Prick the top of the
cupcakes with a toothpick and spoon the melted caramel over the cooled
cupcakes. Then lay slices of apple on top of each cupcake.

apple sauce & brandy drizzle cupcakes
Prepare the basic cupcake recipe. To make the drizzle, combine 4 tablespoons
apple brandy with 3 tablespoons sugar in a medium pan. Simmer gently for
5 minutes, then spoon over the cupcakes. Then lay slices of apple on top of
each cupcake.

variations

peanut butter cupcakes

see base recipe page 36

peanut butter & jam cupcakes
Prepare the basic cupcake recipe. When the cupcakes have cooled, use a sharp knife to slice off the tops. Using a teaspoon, hollow out a small hole in the top of each cupcake. Spoon ½ teaspoon strawberry or raspberry jam into the small hole. Place the top back on the cupcake and ice.

chocolate peanut butter cupcakes
Prepare the basic cupcake recipe. Add 100 g (3½ oz) plain chocolate chips to the batter.

peanut butter cupcakes with fudge-icing
Prepare the basic cupcake recipe. For the icing, substitute smooth peanut butter for the crunchy. Add 2 tablespoons Dutch-process cocoa powder to the icing mixture after adding the milk.

variations

poppy seed cupcakes with lemon drizzle

see base recipe page 37

poppy seed cupcakes with orange & lemon drizzle
Prepare the basic cupcake recipe using ½ tablespoon orange zest and
½ tablespoon lemon zest. To make the drizzle, use only 2 tablespoons
lemon juice and 2 tablespoons orange juice.

poppy seed & blueberry cupcakes with lime drizzle
Prepare the basic cupcake recipe. After creaming the batter, stir in
100 g (3½ oz) blueberries, and substitute 1 tablespoon finely grated
lime zest for the lemon zest.

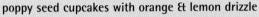

poppy seed & cranberry cupcakes with lemon drizzle
Prepare the basic cupcake recipe. After creaming the batter, stir
100 g (3½ oz) dried chopped cranberries.

banana cupcakes

see base recipe page 39

chocolate chip & banana cupcakes
Prepare the basic cupcake recipe. Stir in 100 g (3½ oz) plain chocolate chips along with the mashed bananas.

cinnamon & oat-topped banana cupcakes
Prepare the basic cupcake recipe. Place 3 tablespoons granulated sugar, 1 teaspoon cinnamon, 2 tablespoons softened unsalted butter, 4 tablespoons porridge oats and 1 tablespoon flour in a medium bowl. Mix until well combined. Sprinkle a little over the cupcakes before baking them.

walnut & cinnamon-iced banana cupcakes
Prepare the basic cupcake recipe. Add 3 tablespoons chopped walnuts and 1 teaspoon cinnamon to the icing after creaming it.

variations

madeleines

see base recipe page 40

cassis-iced madeleines
Prepare the basic recipe. For the icing, add 3 tablespoons cassis liqueur
to the creamed butter and sugar.

chocolate madeleines
Prepare the basic recipe. Substitute 2 tablespoons Dutch-process cocoa
powder for 2 tablespoons of the flour.

vanilla madeleines
Prepare the basic recipe. Add 1 teaspoon vanilla essence to the eggs and
sugar before creaming the batter. Add 1 teaspoon vanilla essence to the
sugar, butter, salt and orange zest before creaming the icing.

fragrant & spiced cupcakes

Exotic and unexpected flavours make these cupcakes a culinary

adventure. Unusual pairings – pistachio and rosewater, fig and

vanilla, cardamom and orange – abound.

carnation cupcakes

see variations page 78

Cooking with flowers goes back centuries. You can find old recipes for flower water, jellies, jams and yes, cupcakes!

for the cupcakes
225 g (8 oz) unsalted butter, softened
225 g (8 oz) caster sugar
225 g (8 oz) self-raising flour
4 eggs
1 tsp vanilla essence

for the icing
200 g (7 oz) icing sugar
2 tbsp lemon juice
3 dozen red, pink or striped carnations

Preheat the oven to 175°C (350°F / Gas mark 4). Place 18 paper baking cases in muffin tins. Combine all the cupcake ingredients in a large bowl and beat with an electric whisk until smooth and pale, about 2 to 3 minutes. Spoon the batter into the cases. Bake for 20 minutes. Remove from the oven and cool for 5 minutes. Remove the cupcakes and cool on a rack.

To make the icing, sieve the icing sugar into a medium bowl. Slowly add the lemon juice, stirring until the icing holds its shape. Spread the icing onto the cooled cupcakes. Snip the stems off the carnation flowers and place a flower in the centre of each cupcake.

Store in an airtight container for up to 3 days, or freeze without icing in an airtight container for up to 3 months.

Makes 1¹/₂ dozen

chai cupcakes

see variations page 79

Chai is a spiced Indian tea made with frothy warm milk — almost like an Indian cappuccino! This cupcake captures its light, spicy flavour.

for the cupcakes
225 g (8 oz) self-raising flour
¼ tsp baking powder
Pinch of salt
1 tbsp chai tea powder
60 g (2½ oz) unsalted butter, softened
150 g (5 oz) light brown sugar
2 egg whites
150 ml (5 fl oz) buttermilk

for the icing
200 g (7 oz) cream cheese, softened
175 g (6 oz) icing sugar, sieved
1 tbsp lemon juice
1 tsp vanilla essence

Preheat the oven to 175°C (350°F / Gas mark 4). Place 12 paper baking cases in a muffin tin. In a medium bowl, mix the flour, baking powder, salt and chai powder. In a separate bowl, beat the butter and sugar until smooth. Add the egg whites slowly, beating well. Slowly add the flour mixture, and finally the buttermilk. Mix until combined. Spoon the batter into the cases. Bake for 20 minutes. Remove tin from the oven and cool for 5 minutes. Then remove the cupcakes and cool on a rack. To make the icing, mix the cream cheese and icing sugar together in a medium bowl and beat until soft and light. Add the lemon and vanilla, and beat until smooth. Spoon the icing over the cupcakes. Store without icing in an airtight container for up to 3 days, or freeze for up to 3 months.

Makes 1 dozen

fennel cupcakes

see variations page 80

Lightly crushed fennel seeds give this cupcake a sweet liquorice flavour. In India, the seeds are chewed after meals to refresh the breath.

for the cupcakes
225 g (8 oz) unsalted butter, softened
225 g (8 oz) caster sugar
225 g (8 oz) self-raising flour
4 eggs
1 tsp finely crushed fennel seeds

for the icing
200 g (7 oz) cream cheese, softened
175 g (6 oz) icing sugar, sieved
1 tbsp liquorice-flavoured liqueur
1 tsp vanilla essence
1 tsp lightly crushed fennel seeds

Preheat the oven to 175°C (350°F / Gas mark 4). Place 18 paper baking cases in muffin tins.

Combine all the cupcake ingredients in a medium bowl and beat with an electric whisk until smooth and pale, about 2 to 3 minutes. Spoon the batter into the cases. Bake for 20 minutes. Remove tins from the oven and cool for 5 minutes. Remove the cupcakes and cool on a rack.

To make the icing, combine the cream cheese and icing sugar, and beat briskly until soft and creamy. Add the liqueur and vanilla, and stir well. Swirl onto the top of the cupcakes and decorate with the fennel seeds.

Store without icing for up to 3 days in an airtight container, or freeze for up to 3 months.

Makes 1 1/2 dozen

rhubarb & ginger cupcakes

see variations page 81

The combination of rhubarb and ginger is magnificent. It is believed that rhubarb originated in China, where it was used for its medicinal properties.

for the cupcakes
225 g (8 oz) unsalted butter, softened
225 g (8 oz) caster sugar
225 g (8 oz) self-raising flour
4 eggs
1 tsp vanilla essence
150 g (5 oz) cooked rhubarb

for the icing
200 g (7 oz) cream cheese, softened
175 g (6 oz) icing sugar, sieved
1 tbsp lime juice
½ tsp ground ginger
1½ tbsp roughly chopped crystallised ginger

Preheat the oven to 200°C (400°F / Gas mark 6). Place 18 paper baking cases in muffin tins. Combine all the cupcake ingredients, except the rhubarb, in a medium bowl and beat with an electric whisk until smooth and pale, about 2 to 3 minutes. Spoon the batter into the cases. Bake for 20 minutes. Remove tins from the oven and cool for 5 minutes. Then remove the cupcakes and cool on a rack. Hollow out a small hole in each cake and fill with 1 teaspoon rhubarb.

For the icing, combine the cream cheese and icing sugar, and beat briskly until soft and creamy. Add the lime juice, ground ginger and crystallised ginger and mix well. Spoon onto the cupcakes. Store without icing in an airtight container for up to 3 days, or freeze for up to 3 months.

Makes 1½ dozen

lavender & honey cupcakes

see variations page 82

The marriage of lavender and honey is truly wonderful. If you can find lavender honey, it will enhance the flavour even more.

for the cupcakes
225 g (8 oz) unsalted butter, softened
225 g (8 oz) caster sugar
225 g (8 oz) self-raising flour
4 eggs
1 tsp vanilla essence

for the icing
200 g (7 oz) cream cheese, softened
175 g (6 oz) icing sugar, sieved
75 g (3 oz) honey
Blue food colouring
2 tbsp dried lavender flowers

Preheat the oven to 200°C (400°F / Gas mark 6). Place 18 baking cases in muffin tins. Combine all the cupcake ingredients in a medium bowl and beat with an electric whisk until smooth and pale, about 2 to 3 minutes. Spoon the batter into the cases. Bake for 20 minutes. Remove tins from the oven and cool for 5 minutes. Then remove the cupcakes and cool on a rack.

For the icing, beat the cream cheese and icing sugar in a medium bowl with an electric whisk, until light and creamy. Beat in the honey and a few drops of the food colouring. Stir in half of the lavender flowers.

Spread the icing onto the cupcakes and sprinkle with the reserved lavender flowers.

Store without icing in an airtight container for up to 3 days, or freeze for up to 3 months.

Makes 1¹/₂ dozen

hummingbird cupcakes with marmalade icing

see variations page 83

The hummingbird cake is a classic recipe from the American South.

for the cupcakes
125 g (4½ oz) plain flour
1 tsp baking powder
½ tsp cinnamon
125 g (4½ oz) caster sugar
115 ml (4 fl oz) safflower oil
2 eggs
150 g (5 oz) mashed bananas
1½ tbsp grated orange zest

60 g (2½ oz) grated carrot
90 g (3¼ oz) tinned pineapple, crushed
60 g (2½ oz) desiccated coconut

for the icing
115 g (4 oz) unsalted butter, softened
150 g (5 oz) icing sugar, sieved
2 tbsp freshly squeezed orange juice
2 tbsp orange marmalade

Preheat the oven to 175°C (350°F / Gas mark 4). Place 12 baking cases in a muffin tin. In a medium bowl, sieve the flour, baking powder and cinnamon. In a large bowl cream the sugar and oil with an electric whisk until light and fluffy. Beat in the eggs slowly, then stir in the dry ingredients in 3 batches. Add the rest of the ingredients, and stir until combined. Spoon the batter into the cases. Bake for 25 minutes. Remove tin from the oven and cool for 5 minutes. Remove the cupcakes and cool on a rack. For the icing, beat the butter in a medium bowl. Add the remaining ingredients. Smear the icing onto the cupcakes. Store without icing in an airtight container for up to 3 days, or freeze for up to 3 months.

Makes 1 dozen

pistachio & rosewater cupcakes

see variations page 84

Rosewater is a delicate, sweet flavouring made by steeping rose petals in water, oil or alcohol. Try to use unsalted pistachios for this recipe.

for the cupcakes
225 g (8 oz) unsalted butter, softened
225 g (8 oz) caster sugar
225 g (8 oz) self-raising flour
4 eggs
1 tsp rosewater

for the icing
200 g (7 oz) cream cheese
175 g (6 oz) icing sugar, sieved
2 tbsp rosewater
3 tbsp chopped pistachios

Preheat the oven to 175°C (350°F / Gas mark 4). Place 18 paper baking cases in muffin tins. Combine all the cupcake ingredients in a medium bowl and beat with an electric whisk until smooth and pale, about 2 to 3 minutes.

Spoon the batter into the cases. Bake for 20 minutes. Remove tins from the oven and cool for 5 minutes. Then remove the cupcakes and cool on a rack.

For the icing, combine the cream cheese and icing sugar, and beat with an electric whisk until soft and creamy. Add the rosewater and pistachios, and stir well. Swirl onto the cupcakes.

Store without icing for up to 3 days in an airtight container, or freeze for up to 3 months.

Makes 1 dozen

orange & armagnac cupcakes

see variations page 85

For adults only! These cupcakes would be ideal on a cold winter night.

for the cupcakes	for the icing
225 g (8 oz) unsalted butter, softened	200 g (7 oz) cream cheese, softened
225 g (8 oz) caster sugar	175 g (6 oz) icing sugar, sieved
225 g (8 oz) self-raising flour	1 tsp orange essence
4 eggs	1½ tbsp grated orange zest
2 tbsp Armagnac	

Preheat the oven to 175°C (350°F / Gas mark 4). Place 18 paper baking cases in muffin tins. Combine all the cupcake ingredients in a medium bowl and beat with an electric whisk until smooth and pale, about 2 to 3 minutes. Spoon the batter into the cases.

Bake for 20 minutes. Remove tins from the oven and cool for 5 minutes. Pierce some holes in the tops of the cupcakes with a skewer and pour ½ tablespoon Armagnac over each one. Then remove the cupcakes and cool on a rack.

To make the icing, beat the cream cheese in a bowl with an electric whisk until light and fluffy. Beat in the icing sugar for 1 to 2 minutes, then beat in the orange essence and zest until smooth and light. Spread the icing on the cupcakes.

Store without icing for up to 2 days in an airtight container, or freeze for up to 3 months.

Makes 1½ dozen

spiced soured cream cupcakes

see variations page 86

The hearty flavour of these cupcakes is perfect for bonfire parties and autumn picnics.

for the cupcakes
190 g (6½ oz) plain flour
1 tsp baking powder
2 tsp cinnamon
1 tsp mixed spice
¼ tsp nutmeg
2 eggs
175 ml (6 fl oz) soured cream
175 g (6 oz) light brown sugar

3 tbsp sultanas
3 tbsp chopped pecans

for the icing
200 g (7 oz) cream cheese, softened
115 g (4 oz) unsalted butter, softened
175 g (6 oz) icing sugar, sieved
1 tbsp grated orange zest
2 tbsp orange juice

Preheat the oven to 175°C (350°F / Gas mark 4). Place 18 paper baking cases in muffin tins. Sieve the dry ingredients into a medium bowl and put aside. In a large bowl, beat the eggs and soured cream with an electric whisk. Add the sugar and mix well. Then add the dry ingredients in 3 batches, mixing each batch until smooth. Stir in the sultanas and pecans. Spoon the batter into the cases. Bake for 20 minutes until firm. Remove tins from the oven and cool for 5 minutes. Then remove the cupcakes and cool on a rack. To make the icing, beat the cream cheese and butter together with an electric whisk, until light and fluffy. Add the icing sugar and beat until creamy. Beat in the orange zest and the juice. Spread the icing on the cupcakes. Store without icing in an airtight container for up to 3 days, or freeze for up to 3 months.

Makes 1¹/₂ dozen

cardamom & orange cupcakes

see variations page 87

Cardamom has a pungent aroma and is often used in Indian cooking to flavour curries.

for the cupcakes
225 g (8 oz) unsalted butter, softened
225 g (8 oz) caster sugar
225 g (8 oz) self-raising flour
4 eggs
1 tsp ground cardamom
1 tsp orange essence

for the icing
250 g (9 oz) icing sugar, sieved
115 g (4 oz) unsalted butter, softened
50 ml (2 fl oz) soured cream
1½ tbsp grated orange zest
1 tsp orange essence
36 cardamom pods (for decoration only)

Preheat the oven to 175°C (350°F / Gas mark 4). Place 18 paper baking cases in muffin tins. Combine all the cupcake ingredients in a medium bowl and beat with an electric whisk until smooth and pale, about 2 to 3 minutes.

Spoon the batter into the cases. Bake in the oven for 20 minutes. Remove tins from the oven and cool for 5 minutes. Then remove the cupcakes and cool on a rack.

To make the icing, beat the icing sugar, butter, soured cream, orange zest and orange essence with an electric whisk until smooth. Spread the icing on the cupcakes and top each with 2 cardamom pods. Store without icing for up to 2 days in an airtight container, or freeze for up to 3 months.

Makes 1¹/₂ dozen

courgette & feta muffins

see variations page 88

These savoury muffins offer a flavour of the Mediterranean. You'll find courgettes and feta combined in Greek and Turkish salads, alongside plump olives and flatbreads.

250 g (9 oz) plain flour
1 tbsp baking powder
Pinch of salt
2 eggs
115 ml (4 fl oz) virgin olive oil

175 g (6 oz) grated courgettes
115 g (4 oz) crumbled feta cheese
1½ tbsp grated lemon zest

Preheat the oven to 175°C (350°F / Gas mark 4). Grease a 6-cup muffin tin.

Sieve the dry ingredients together in a medium bowl.

In a large bowl, beat the eggs and oil with an electric whisk until smooth. Stir in the courgettes, feta cheese and lemon zest. Add the dry ingredients, and stir until the mixture is just combined.

Spoon the mixture into the prepared tin. Bake for 30 minutes. Remove tin from the oven and cool for 5 minutes. Remove the muffins and cool on a rack.

Store refrigerated in an airtight container for up to 2 days, or freeze for up to 3 months.

Makes ½ dozen

fig & vanilla cupcakes

see variations page 89

Dried figs are sweeter than fresh figs. Indeed, the Romans used dried figs as sweeteners because cane sugar was so rare and expensive.

for the cupcakes
225 g (8 oz) unsalted butter, softened
225 g (8 oz) caster sugar
225 g (8 oz) self-raising flour
1 tsp baking powder
4 eggs
1 tbsp vanilla essence
150 g (5 oz) finely chopped dried figs

for the icing
200 g (7 oz) cream cheese, softened
175 g (6 oz) icing sugar, sieved
1 tsp vanilla essence
1 tbsp grated lemon zest
3 tbsp chopped figs

Preheat the oven to 175°C (350°F / Gas mark 4). Place 18 baking cases in muffin tins. Combine all the cupcake ingredients in a large bowl and beat with an electric whisk until smooth and pale, about 2 to 3 minutes.

Spoon the batter into the cases. Bake for 20 minutes. Remove tins from the oven and cool for 5 minutes. Then remove the cupcakes and cool on a rack.

To make the icing, beat the cream cheese, icing sugar, vanilla and lemon zest with an electric whisk until soft and creamy. Smear the cupcakes with the icing. Store without icing in an airtight container for up to 2 days, or freeze for up to 3 months.

Makes 1 1/2 dozen

variations

carnation cupcakes

see base recipe page 57

frosted flower cupcakes
Prepare the basic cupcake recipe. To prepare the frosted flowers, put an egg white in a small bowl and some granulated sugar in another small bowl. Take a selection of flower petals (roses and pansies work well) and brush with egg white on both sides. Dust the petals with the sugar, place on a tray and leave in a cool dry place to dry and stiffen. Lay on top of the iced cupcakes.

rose cupcakes
Prepare the basic cupcake recipe. Substitute 2 dozen rose petals for the carnations.

citrus cream carnation cupcakes
Prepare the basic cupcake recipe. To make a citrus cream icing, combine 100 g (3½ oz) cream cheese with 2 teaspoons orange and lemon zest in a small bowl. Stir in 3 tablespoons icing sugar, spread onto the cupcakes and garnish with the carnations.

variations

chai cupcakes

see base recipe page 58

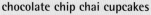

chocolate chip chai cupcakes
Prepare the basic cupcake recipe, stirring in 100 g (3½ oz) plain chocolate chips after adding the buttermilk.

cinnamon & orange chai cupcakes
Prepare the basic cupcake recipe, adding 2 teaspoons cinnamon to the dry ingredients. Add 1 tablespoon grated orange zest along with the buttermilk.

white chocolate & vanilla chai cupcakes
Prepare the basic cupcake recipe. Add 100 g (3½ oz) white chocolate chips and 1 teaspoon vanilla essence after adding the buttermilk.

variations

fennel cupcakes

see base recipe page 61

fennel & orange cupcakes
Prepare the basic cupcake recipe. Add 1 tablespoon finely grated orange zest to the cupcake mixture. For the icing, substitute 1 teaspoon orange essence for the vanilla.

fennel & almond cupcakes
Prepare the basic cupcake recipe, adding 4 tablespoons chopped blanched almonds after mixing the cupcake batter.

fennel & pink pepper cupcakes
Prepare the basic cupcake recipe. For the icing, omit the vanilla essence and instead add 1 teaspoon finely crushed pink peppercorns.

variations

rhubarb & ginger cupcakes

see base recipe page 62

rhubarb & cinnamon cupcakes
Prepare the basic cupcake recipe. Add 2 teaspoons cinnamon to the cupcake mixture before stirring the batter.

rhubarb & custard cupcakes
Prepare the basic cupcake recipe. Slice the cupcakes horizontally and spread 1 tablespoon custard onto the base. Pop the top back on and smother with the ginger icing.

sultana, rhubarb & ginger cupcakes
Prepare the basic cupcake recipe. After mixing the batter, add 60 g (2½ oz) sultanas.

variations

lavender & honey cupcakes

see base recipe page 65

dark chocolate & lavender cupcakes
Prepare the basic cupcake recipe. After mixing the batter, fold in 100 g
(3½ oz) plain dark chocolate chips.

gumdrop & lavender cupcakes
Prepare the basic cupcake recipe. After mixing the batter, fold in 100 g
(3½ oz) mixed fruit gumdrops to the batter.

lavender & orange flower cream cupcakes
Prepare the basic cupcake recipe. To make the icing, combine 3 tablespoons
orange flower water with the cream cheese and icing sugar. Beat well and
stir in the lavender flowers.

hummingbird cupcakes with marmalade icing

see base recipe page 66

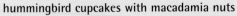

hummingbird cupcakes with macadamia nuts
Prepare the basic cupcake recipe adding 100 g (3½ oz) chopped
macadamia nuts after mixing in the eggs.

hummingbird cupcakes with figs
Prepare the basic cupcake recipe, substituting 90 g (3¼ oz) chopped
dried figs for the pineapple.

hummingird cupcakes with lemon icing
Prepare the basic cupcake recipe. To make the icing, substitute
2 tablespoons lemon juice for the orange juice, and 2 tablespoons
lemon curd for the marmalade.

variations

pistachio & rosewater cupcakes

see base recipe page 69

pomegranate & rosewater cupcakes
Prepare the basic cupcake recipe. For the icing, add 3 tablespoons pomegranate seeds after combining the cream cheese and icing sugar.

walnut & rosewater cupcakes
Prepare the basic cupcake recipe. For the icing, substitute 3 tablespoons chopped walnuts for the pistachios.

almond & rosewater cupcakes
Prepare the basic cupcake recipe. For the icing, substitute 3 tablespoons toasted almonds for the pistachios.

orange & armagnac cupcakes

see base recipe page 70

chocolate chip & armagnac cupcakes
Prepare the basic cupcake recipe, adding 100 g (3½ oz) plain chocolate chips after combining the rest of the cupcake ingredients.

almond & amaretto cupcakes
Prepare the basic cupcake recipe, substituting 2 tablespoons Amaretto for the Armagnac. Add 3 tablespoons ground almonds to the cupcake mixture along with the other ingredients. For the icing, add 2 tablespoons chopped almonds, and omit the orange juice and zest.

hazelnut & kahlua cupcakes
Prepare the basic cupcake recipe, substituting 2 tablespoons Kahlua for the Armagnac. Add 3 tablespoons finely chopped hazelnuts to the cupcake mixture along with the other ingredients. For the icing, add 2 tablespoons chopped hazelnuts, and omit the orange juice and zest.

variations

spiced soured cream cupcakes

see base recipe page 71

spiced ginger-iced cupcakes
Prepare the basic cupcake recipe. For the icing, substitute 3 tablespoons chopped crystallised ginger for the orange zest and orange juice.

spiced coffee-iced cupcakes
Prepare the basic cupcake recipe. To make the icing, mix 2 tablespoons strong coffee and 2 tablespoons malted milk powder until dissolved. Whisk 175 g (6 oz) icing sugar into the coffee mixture until dissolved.

spiced maple & walnut-iced cupcakes
Prepare the basic cupcake recipe. To make the icing, add ½ teaspoon maple-flavoured essence to the creamed icing sugar, butter and cream cheese. Omit the orange juice and zest. Smear the icing onto the cupcakes and top with 100 g (3½ oz) chopped walnuts.

variations

cardamom & orange cupcakes

see base recipe page 73

coffee-iced cardamom cupcakes
Prepare the basic cupcake recipe. For the icing, omit the orange zest and
essence. Add 2 tablespoons instant coffee granules to 1 teaspoon hot
coffee. Stir to dissolve. Stir in 1 tablespoon Kahlua. Set aside to cool.
Stir the cooled coffee mixture into the creamed icing sugar, butter and
soured cream.

cardamom custard cupcakes
Prepare the basic cupcake recipe. Slice the cupcakes horizontally and
spread 1 tablespoon custard onto the base. Pop the top back on and
smother with the orange icing.

cardamom & lemongrass cupcakes
Prepare the basic cupcake recipe. For the icing, add 1 tablespoon
finely chopped lemongrass after creaming the other ingredients.

variations

courgette & feta muffins

see base recipe page 74

courgette & carrot muffins
Prepare the basic muffin recipe, substituting 90 g (3¼ oz) finely grated carrot for 90 g (3¼ oz) grated courgettes.

courgette, feta & olive muffins
Prepare the basic muffin recipe, adding 3 tablespoons finely chopped olives to the muffin batter.

courgette & orange muffins
Prepare the basic muffin recipe, adding 1 tablespoon finely grated orange zest to the muffin batter.

variations

fig & vanilla cupcakes

see base recipe page 77

orange-iced fig & vanilla cupcakes
Prepare the basic cupcake recipe. In the icing, add 2 tablespoons orange marmalade and substitute 1 tablespoon orange zest for the lemon zest.

fig & vanilla cupcakes with honey buttercream
Prepare the basic cupcake recipe. For the icing, add 75 g (3 oz) honey after creaming the cream cheese and icing sugar.

ginger-iced fig & vanilla cupcakes
Prepare the basic cupcake recipe. For the icing, add 1 teaspoon ground ginger and 60 g (2½ oz) crystallised ginger after combining the cream cheese and icing sugar.

chocolate cupcakes

Minted chocolate cupcakes, chocolate chip and raisin brioches,

white chocolate and strawberry cupcakes – the cupcakes in this

chapter will satisfy your chocolate craving in an instant!

chocolate mud cupcakes

see variations page 111

These cupcakes are so simple to make you won't hesitate to make another batch!

300 g (10½ oz) plain chocolate chips
300 g (10½ oz) unsalted butter
5 eggs

115 g (4 oz) caster sugar
115 g (4 oz) self-raising flour
2 tbsp Dutch-process cocoa powder, for dusting

Preheat the oven to 160°C (325°F / Gas mark 3). Place 12 paper baking cases in a muffin tin.

In a medium bowl set over a pan of gently simmering water, melt the chocolate and butter together, stirring well. Leave to cool a little.

Beat the eggs and sugar in a large bowl until pale and thick. Fold the flour into the egg mixture and then stir in the melted chocolate and butter until well blended.

Spoon the mixture into the cases and bake for 20 minutes. The cupcakes will be soft and gooey in texture and appearance. Remove tin from the oven and cool for 5 minutes. Then remove the cupcakes and serve swiftly, dusted with cocoa powder.

Store in the refrigerator in an airtight container for up to 3 days.

Makes 1 dozen

chocolate ice cream cupcakes

see variations page 112

It's best to move these cupcakes from freezer to refrigerator 30 minutes before serving.

for the cupcakes
225 g (8 oz) unsalted butter, softened
225 g (8 oz) caster sugar
225 g (8 oz) self-raising flour
4 tbsp Dutch-process cocoa powder
1 tsp baking powder
4 eggs
1 tsp vanilla essence

for the filling and glaze
175 g (6 oz) chocolate ice cream
100 g (3½ oz) plain chocolate chips
75 ml (3 fl oz) whipping cream

Preheat the oven to 175°C (350°F / Gas mark 4). Place 18 paper baking cases in muffin tins. Combine all the cupcake ingredients in a medium bowl and beat with an electric whisk until smooth and creamy, about 2 to 3 minutes.

Spoon the batter into the cases. Bake for 20 minutes. Remove tins from the oven and cool for 5 minutes. Then remove the cupcakes and cool on a rack. When cool, slice the cupcakes horizontally and spread a little softened ice cream on the bottom slice. Place the top back on the cupcake and freeze. Prepare the glaze by melting the chocolate in a medium bowl over a pan of simmering water, stirring until completely melted. Remove from the heat. Add the cream and stir until well combined. Cool slightly and spoon over the cupcakes. Return to the freezer to set. Freeze in an airtight container for up to 3 months.

Makes 1½ dozen

chocolate brownie cupcakes

see variations page 113

Serve these warm from the oven, topped with a generous spoonful of vanilla cream.

for the cupcakes
125 g (4½ oz) plain chocolate chips
125 g (4½ oz) unsalted butter
2 eggs
300 g (10½ oz) caster sugar
1 tsp vanilla essence
115 g (4 oz) plain flour

for the topping
225 ml (8 fl oz) whipping cream
1 tsp vanilla essence
3 tbsp icing sugar, sieved

Preheat the oven to 160°C (325°F / Gas mark 3). Place 12 paper baking cases in a muffin tin. Melt the chocolate and butter in a medium bowl over a pan of simmering water, stirring until melted. Set aside to cool. In a medium bowl, beat the eggs, sugar, and vanilla until pale and thick. Fold in the chocolate and then the flour, mixing until well combined.

Spoon batter into the cases. Bake for 25 minutes. Remove tin from the oven and cool for 5 minutes. Then remove the cupcakes and cool on a rack.

For the topping, beat the cream in a medium bowl until semi-stiff. Fold in the vanilla and icing sugar. Place a dollop or two on each brownie.

Store without topping in an airtight container for up to 2 days.

Makes 1 dozen

white chocolate &
strawberry cupcakes

see variations page 114

Simple yet sophisticated – and perfect for a summer picnic!

for the cupcakes
225 g (8 oz) unsalted butter, softened
225 g (8 oz) caster sugar
225 g (8 oz) self-raising flour
1 tsp baking powder
4 eggs
1 tsp strawberry essence
100 g (3½ oz) white chocolate chips

for the icing
200 g (7 oz) cream cheese, softened
175 g (6 oz) icing sugar, sieved
1 tsp vanilla essence
3 tbsp unsalted butter, softened
3 tbsp chopped fresh strawberries

Preheat the oven to 175°C (350°F / Gas mark 4). Place 18 paper baking cases in muffin tins. Combine the butter, sugar, flour, baking powder, eggs and strawberry essence in a medium bowl. Beat with an electric whisk until light and creamy, about 2 to 3 minutes. Stir in the chocolate chips. Spoon the batter into the cases. Bake for 20 minutes. Remove tins from the oven and cool for 5 minutes. Then remove the cupcakes and cool on a rack. To make the icing, beat the cream cheese, icing sugar, vanilla and butter until smooth and creamy. Stir in the chopped strawberries. Spread on top of the cupcakes.

Store without icing in an airtight container for up to 2 days, or freeze for up to 3 months.

Makes 1½ dozen

chocolate & chilli cupcakes

see variations page 115

The Spanish *conquistadors* brought chocolate back from Mexico, a fact that inspired this delicious combination of dark chocolate and tingling chilli.

for the cupcakes
225 g (8 oz) unsalted butter, softened
225 g (8 oz) caster sugar
225 g (8 oz) self-raising flour
4 tbsp Dutch-process cocoa powder
1 tsp baking powder
4 eggs
2 tsp chilli powder
100 g (3½ oz) plain dark chocolate chips

for the icing
175 g (6 oz) icing sugar, sieved
50 g (2 oz) Dutch-process cocoa powder
3 tbsp Tia Maria
115 g (4 oz) unsalted butter, softened

Preheat the oven to 175°C (350°F / Gas mark 4). Place 18 paper baking cases in muffin tins. Combine all the cupcake ingredients, except the chocolate chips, in a large bowl and beat with an electric whisk until smooth, about 2 to 3 minutes. Stir in the chocolate chips.

Spoon the batter into the cases. Bake for 20 minutes. Remove tins from the oven and cool for 5 minutes. Then remove the cupcakes and cool on a rack. To make the icing, blend all the ingredients together in a food processor. Spread the icing on the cooled cupcakes.

Store without icing in an airtight container for up to 2 days.

Makes 1½ dozen

white chocolate & macadamia nut cupcakes

see variations page 116

Technically, white chocolate is not a chocolate, but it tastes just as decadent!

for the cupcakes
225 g (8 oz) unsalted butter, softened
225 g (8 oz) caster sugar
225 g (8 oz) self-raising flour
1 tsp baking powder
4 eggs
1 tsp vanilla essence
100 g (3½ oz) white chocolate chips

for the icing
200 g (7 oz) white chocolate chips
5 tbsp milk
175 g (6 oz) icing sugar, sieved
3 tbsp chopped toasted macadamia nuts

Preheat the oven to 175°C (350°F / Gas mark 4). Place 18 paper baking cases in muffin tins. Combine all the cupcake ingredients, except the chocolate chips, in a large bowl and beat with an electric whisk until smooth and pale, about 2 to 3 minutes. Stir in the chocolate chips.

Spoon the batter into the cases. Bake for 20 minutes. Remove tins from the oven and cool for 5 minutes. Then remove the cupcakes and cool on a rack. To make the icing, melt the chocolate and milk in a medium bowl over a pan of simmering water, stirring frequently. Remove from the heat and beat in the icing sugar until smooth. Spread over the cupcakes and sprinkle with the nuts. Store in an airtight container for up to 2 days.

Makes 1½ dozen

choc fudge-iced cupcakes

see variations page 117

This fudge icing is bound to bring even the mildest chocaholics to their knees!

for the cupcakes
225 g (8 oz) unsalted butter, softened
225 g (8 oz) caster sugar
225 g (8 oz) self-raising flour
1 tsp baking powder
4 eggs
1 tsp vanilla essence

for the icing
100g (3½ oz) dark chocolate, roughly chopped
2 tbsp milk
50 g (2 oz) unsalted butter
90 g (3¼ oz) icing sugar, sieved

Preheat the oven to 175˚C (350˚F / Gas mark 4). Place 18 paper baking cases into muffin tins. Combine all the cupcake ingredients in a medium bowl and beat with an electric whisk until smooth and pale, about 2 to 3 minutes. Spoon the batter into the cases. Bake for 20 minutes. Remove the tins from the oven and cool for 5 minutes. Then remove the cupcakes and cool on the rack.

To make the icing, gently heat the chocolate, milk and butter in a small, heavy-based saucepan, stirring until melted. Remove from the heat and beat in the icing sugar. Swirl the icing onto the cooled cupcakes.

Store without icing in an airtight container for up to 3 days, or freeze for up to 3 months.

Makes 1½ dozen

devil's food cupcakes

see variations page 118

These cupcakes are incredibly rich and moist delights!

for the cupcakes
225 g (8 oz) self-raising flour
1 tsp baking powder
225 g (8 oz) light brown sugar
225 g (8 oz) unsalted butter, softened
2 separated eggs
100 g (3½ oz) plain chocolate, melted
1 tsp vanilla essence
115 ml (4 fl oz) milk

for the icing
115 g (4 oz) unsalted butter, softened
1 tbsp milk
115 g (4 oz) plain dark chocolate, melted
1 tsp vanilla essence
90 g (3¼ oz) icing sugar, sieved

Preheat the oven to 175°C (350°F / Gas mark 4). Place 18 paper baking cases into muffin tins. Sieve the flour and baking powder and set aside. In a medium bowl, cream the sugar and butter. Add the egg yolks and beat well. Add the melted chocolate and vanilla, mixing well. Add the flour and milk alternately, beating well with each addition. Beat the egg whites in a medium bowl until soft peaks form, and gently fold them into the batter.

Spoon the batter into the cases. Bake for 20 minutes. Remove tins from the oven and cool for 5 minutes. Then remove the cupcakes and cool on a rack. To make the icing, cream the butter in a medium bowl. Beat in the milk until smooth. Stir in the chocolate and vanilla. Beat in the icing sugar until thick and creamy. Spread over the cupcakes. Store without icing in an airtight container for up to 2 days, or freeze for up to 3 months.

Makes 1½ dozen

choc 'n' cherry cupcakes

see variations page 119

The classic German "Black Forest Gâteau" was the inspiration for this cupcake.

for the cupcakes
225 g (8 oz) self-raising flour
4 tbsp Dutch-process cocoa powder
1 tsp baking powder
225 g (8 oz) caster sugar
225 g (8 oz) unsalted butter, softened
4 eggs
90 g (3¼ oz) chopped cherries
2 tbsp kirsch (or other cherry-flavoured liqueur)

for the topping
200 ml (7 fl oz) whipping cream
3 tbsp icing sugar, sieved
12 whole cherries
100 g (3½ oz) dark chocolate bar

Preheat the oven to 160°C (325°F / Gas mark 3). Place 18 paper baking cases in muffin tins. In a medium bowl, sieve the flour, cocoa, and baking powder. Set aside. Cream the sugar and butter in a large bowl until smooth. Add the eggs one at a time, beating well with each addition. Add the flour mixture and the cherries, and stir until well combined. Spoon the batter into the cases. Bake for 20 minutes. Remove tins from the oven and cool for 5 minutes. Pour a little kirsch over each cupcake. Remove the cupcakes from the tins and cool on a rack. For the topping, whip the cream and icing sugar together until slightly stiff. Using a vegetable peeler, shave curls of chocolate from the bar. Garnish the cupcakes with a dollop of cream. Place a cherry in the centre, and chocolate around it. Store without icing in an airtight container for up to 3 days.

Makes 1½ dozen

mint chocolate cupcakes

see variations page 120

Mint is a versatile herb that complements both sweet and savoury dishes.

for the cupcakes
225 g (8 oz) self-raising flour
4 tbsp Dutch-process cocoa powder
1 tsp baking powder
225 g (8 oz) caster sugar
225 g (8 oz) unsalted butter, softened
4 eggs
1 tsp mint essence
100 g (3½ oz) plain chocolate chips

for the icing
115 g (4 oz) unsalted butter, softened
225 g (8 oz) icing sugar, sieved
1 tsp mint essence
Green food colouring
100 g (3½ oz) plain chocolate chips

Preheat the oven to 160°C (325°F / Gas mark 3). Place 18 paper baking cases into muffin tins. In a medium bowl, sieve the flour, cocoa, and baking powder. Set aside. Beat the sugar and butter together in a large bowl until smooth. Add the eggs one at a time, beating well after each addition. Add the flour mixture gradually, stirring until well combined. Stir in the mint essence and chocolate chips. Spoon the mixture into the cases. Bake for 20 minutes. Remove the tins from the oven and cool for 5 minutes. Then remove the cupcakes and cool on a rack. To make the icing, beat the butter and icing sugar in a small bowl until smooth and creamy. Stir in the mint essence and just enough food colouring to turn the icing a mint green. Ice the cupcakes and decorate with chocolate chips. Store without icing in an airtight container for up to 3 days, or freeze for up to 3 months.

Makes 1½ dozen

chocolate chip & raisin brioches

see variations page 121

You'll find yourself drawn to the breakfast table by the aroma of these sweet breads, a perfect accompaniment to steaming hot coffee.

½ tbsp active dried yeast
115 ml (4 fl oz) warm water
1 tsp sugar
275 g (10 oz) plain flour
4 eggs
60 g (2½ oz) caster sugar

Pinch of salt
115 g (4 oz) unsalted butter, softened
90 g (3¼ oz) raisins
115 g (4 oz) plain chocolate chips
1 beaten egg

Combine the yeast, water and the teaspoon of sugar in a large bowl. Stir well and leave in a warm place for 10 minutes. Stir in 100 g (3½ oz) of the flour until the mixture becomes a smooth paste. Beat the eggs and add them to the yeast mixture. Add the sugar and salt. Stir in the remaining flour, and mix until the dough is soft and slightly sticky. Leave in a warm place, covered with cling film, for 45 minutes or until doubled in bulk. Preheat the oven to 200°C (400°F / Gas mark 6). Grease 12 mini brioche or muffin moulds. Beat in the butter, raisins and chocolate chips. Fill the moulds halfway. Leave in a warm place to rise for about 20 minutes, until the dough has risen to fill about two-thirds each mould.

Brush each brioche with a little of the beaten egg and bake for 20 minutes. Cool in the moulds for 5 minutes, remove and cool on a rack. Store in an airtight container for up to 2 days.

Makes 1 dozen

chocolate hazelnut cupcakes

see variations page 122

A timeless combination . . . with very little flour in the mix!

115 g (4 oz) unsalted butter
115 g (4 oz) plain chocolate chips
115 g (4 oz) caster sugar

4 separated eggs
2 tbsp plain flour
50 g (2 oz) chopped, roasted hazelnuts

Preheat the oven to 160°C (325°F / Gas mark 3). Place 12 paper baking cases in a muffin tin. Melt the butter and chocolate in a medium bowl over a pan of simmering water, stirring until completely melted. Cool slightly.

Beat the sugar and egg yolks in a medium bowl until thick and creamy. Stir the melted chocolate, flour and hazelnuts into the egg mixture.

In a medium bowl, beat the egg whites to soft peaks, and gently fold into the chocolate mixture. Spoon the batter into the cases.

Bake for 20 minutes. Remove tin from the oven and cool for 5 minutes. Then remove the cupcakes and cool on a rack.

Store refrigerated in an airtight container for up to 2 days, or freeze for up to 3 months.

Makes 1 dozen

chocolate orange cupcakes

see variations page 123

Orange essence helps sweeten the bitterness of the chocolate.

for the cupcakes
225 g (8 oz) unsalted butter, softened
225 g (8 oz) caster sugar
225 g (8 oz) self-raising flour
1 tsp baking powder
4 eggs
1 tsp orange essence

1½ tbsp grated orange zest
100 g (3½ oz) plain dark chocolate chips

for the glaze
100 g (3½ oz) plain dark chocolate chips
75 ml (3 fl oz) whipping cream
1 tsp orange essence

Preheat the oven to 175°C (350°F / Gas mark 4). Place 18 paper baking cases into muffin tins. Combine all the cupcake ingredients, except the chocolate chips, in a large bowl and beat with an electric whisk until smooth and pale, about 2 to 3 minutes. Stir in the chocolate chips.

Spoon the batter into the cases. Bake for 20 minutes. Remove tins from the oven and cool for 5 minutes. Then remove the cupcakes and cool on a rack.

For the chocolate glaze, melt the chocolate in a medium bowl over a pan of simmering water, stirring until completely melted. Add the cream and orange essence, and stir until well combined. Cool slightly and pour over the cupcakes. Refrigerate until set.

Store unglazed in an airtight container for up to 2 days, or freeze for up to 3 months.

Makes 1½ dozen

variations

chocolate mud cupcakes

see base recipe page 91

raspberry mud cupcakes
Prepare the basic cupcake recipe. Stir in 100 g (3½ oz) lightly crushed
raspberries to the mixture after adding the melted chocolate.

white chocolate mud cupcakes
Prepare the basic cupcake recipe. Substitute 100 g (3½ oz) white chocolate
chips for the plain chocolate chips.

macadamia mud cupcakes
Prepare the basic cupcake recipe. Toast and chop 100 g (3½ oz) macadamia
nuts, and stir them in after adding the melted chocolate.

variations

chocolate ice cream cupcakes

see base recipe page 92

vanilla ice cream cupcakes
Prepare the basic cupcake recipe, substituting 175 g (6 oz) vanilla ice cream for the chocolate ice cream.

chocolate chip & mint ice cream cupcakes
Prepare the basic cupcake recipe, substituting 175 g (6 oz) mint chocolate chip ice cream for the chocolate ice cream.

caramel ice cream cupcakes
Prepare the basic cupcake recipe, substituting 175 g (6 oz) caramel ice cream for the chocolate ice cream.

variations

chocolate brownie cupcakes

see base recipe page 94

pecan brownie cupcakes
Prepare the basic cupcake recipe. Stir 100 g (3½ oz) chopped pecans into the mixture with the chocolate chips.

dalmatian brownie cupcakes
Prepare the basic cupcake recipe, substituting white chocolate chips for half the quantity of plain chocolate chips.

chocolate fudge-iced brownie cupcakes
Prepare the basic cupcake recipe. To make the icing, combine 100 g (3½ oz) plain chocolate, 2 tablespoons milk and 4 tablespoons unsalted butter in a medium saucepan and stir until the chocolate has melted. Cool slightly and add the icing sugar. Mix until smooth.

variations

white chocolate & strawberry cupcakes

see base recipe page 95

chocolate & black pepper cupcakes
Prepare the basic cupcake recipe, but replace the white chocolate chips with plain chocolate chips. Stir in 1 teaspoon freshly ground black pepper.

balsamic vinegar & strawberry cupcakes
Prepare the basic cupcake recipe, substituting 2 teaspoons sweet balsamic vinegar for the vanilla essence. Omit the white chocolate chips.

white chocolate & raspberry cupcakes
Prepare the basic cupcake recipe, using 150 g (5 oz) fresh or thawed frozen raspberries instead of strawberries.

variations

chocolate & chilli cupcakes

see base recipe page 96

white chocolate & chilli cupcakes
Prepare the basic cupcake recipe, substituting white chocolate chips for
the plain dark chocolate chips.

vodka-iced chocolate & chilli cupcakes
Prepare the basic cupcake recipe. For the icing, substitute 3 tablespoons
vodka for the Tia Maria.

orange liqueur-iced chocolate & chilli cupcakes
Prepare the basic cupcake recipe. For the icing, substitute 3 tablespoons
Grand Marnier or another orange liqueur for the Tia Maria.

white chocolate & macadamia nut cupcakes

see base recipe page 99

white chocolate & apricot cupcakes
Prepare the basic cupcake recipe, substituting 50 g (2 oz) finely chopped dried apricots for half the white chocolate chips.

white chocolate & almond cupcakes
Prepare the basic cupcake recipe, substituting 50 g (2 oz) chopped blanched almonds for half the white chocolate chips. For the icing, substitute 3 tablespoons toasted almonds for the macadamia nuts.

cranberry, orange & macadamia nut cupcakes
Prepare the basic cupcake recipe, using only 50 g (2 oz) white chocolate chips and adding 50 g (2 oz) dried cranberries and 1 tablespoon orange zest.

variations

choc fudge-iced cupcakes

see base recipe page 100

smartie fudge-iced cupcakes
Prepare the basic cupcake recipe. For the frosting, add 100 g (3½ oz) lightly crushed smarties to the mixture after creaming the other ingredients.

white chocolate fudge-iced cupcakes
Prepare the basic cupcake recipe. For the frosting, substitute 100 g (3½ oz) white chocolate for the plain chocolate and add 1 teaspoon vanilla essence.

fudge-iced sultana cupcakes
Prepare the basic cupcake recipe, and add 75 g (3 oz) sultanas to the mixture after creaming the batter.

variations

devil's food cupcakes

see base recipe page 101

coffee-iced devil's cupcakes
Prepare the basic cupcake recipe. For the icing, mix 1 teaspoon hot coffee with 2 tablespoons coffee granules and stir until dissolved. Leave to cool. Stir the cooled coffee into the chocolate icing.

white chocolate-iced devil's cupcakes
Prepare the basic cupcake recipe. For the icing, substitute 100 g (3½ oz) melted white chocolate for the plain chocolate.

hazelnut & chocolate-iced devil's cupcakes
Prepare the basic cupcake recipe. For the icing, add 100 g (3½ oz) chopped toasted hazelnuts after combining the other ingredients.

choc 'n' cherry cupcakes

see base recipe page 103

flaked almond 'n' cherry cupcakes
Prepare the basic cupcake recipe, folding 3 tablespoons toasted flaked almonds into the cream after it has been whipped.

choc 'n' prune cupcakes
Prepare the basic cupcake recipe, substituting 90 g (3¼ oz) chopped prunes for the cherries. For the icing, substitute 3 tablespoons chopped prunes for the whole cherries.

choc 'n' blueberry cupcakes
Prepare the basic cupcake recipe, substituting 90 g (3¼ oz) chopped crushed blueberries for the cherries. For the icing, substitute 3 tablespoons blueberries for the cherries.

variations

mint chocolate cupcakes

see base recipe page 104

sultana & mint chocolate cupcakes
Prepare the basic cupcake recipe, adding 100 g (3½ oz) sultanas along with the chocolate chips.

extra minty cupcakes
Prepare the basic cupcake recipe, substituting 100 g (3½ oz) mint chocolate chips for the plain chocolate chips.

orange & mint cupcakes
Prepare the basic cupcake recipe, substituting 100 g (3½ oz) orange chocolate chunks for the plain chocolate chips.

chocolate chip & raisin brioches

see base recipe page 107

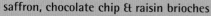

saffron, chocolate chip & raisin brioches
Prepare the basic cupcake recipe, adding a pinch of saffron to the
dry ingredients.

white chocolate & macadamia nut brioches
Prepare the basic cupcake recipe, substituting 90 g (3¼ oz) white chocolate
chips and 115 g (4 oz) chopped macadamia nuts for the chocolate chips
and raisins.

chocolate & cinnamon brioches
Prepare the basic cupcake recipe, adding 2 teaspoons cinnamon to the flour.

variations

chocolate hazelnut cupcakes

see base recipe page 108

chocolate hazelnut & cranberry cupcakes
Prepare the basic cupcake recipe, adding 3 tablespoons chopped dried cranberries to the egg mixture.

chocolate hazelnut & orange cupcakes
Prepare the basic cupcake recipe, adding 2 tablespoons finely grated orange zest to the egg mixture.

chocolate macadamia nut cupcakes
Prepare the basic cupcake recipe, substituting 100 g (3½ oz) roasted and chopped macadamia nuts for the hazelnuts.

chocolate orange cupcakes

see base recipe page 110

chocolate orange marshmallow-centred cupcakes
Bake and cool the cupcakes. Slice the top off each cupcake and hollow out a small hole. Push 1 miniature marshmallow into the hole. Place the "lid" back on and ice with the chocolate glaze.

chocolate orange & vanilla custard cupcakes
Bake and cool the cupcakes. Slice the top off each cupcake and hollow out a small hole. Pipe 1 teaspoon vanilla custard into the hole. Replace the "lid" and ice with the chocolate glaze.

white chocolate & vanilla cupcakes
Prepare the basic cupcake recipe, substituting white chocolate chips for the plain dark chocolate chips and vanilla essence for the orange essence. Omit the orange zest. Use white chocolate chips for the glaze instead of plain dark chocolate.

decadent cupcakes

The recipes in this chapter will leave no doubt in your mind that

the cupcake is most definitely a grown-up treat. From baked

cheesecakes to brioche bread pudding to Florentine cupcakes,

this chapter provides luxurious desserts in individual-size portions!

florentine cupcakes

see variations page 146

Savour *la dolce vita* when you bite into these Italian-inspired cupcakes.

for the cupcakes
225 g (8 oz) unsalted butter, softened
225 g (8 oz) caster sugar
225 g (8 oz) self-raising flour
4 eggs
1 tsp vanilla essence

for the topping
3 tbsp flaked almonds
3 tbsp corn flakes
3 tbsp roughly chopped glacé cherries
3 tbsp sultanas
5 tbsp condensed milk
50 g (2 oz) plain chocolate, melted
50 g (2 oz) white chocolate, melted

Preheat the oven to 175°C (350°F / Gas mark 4). Place 18 paper baking cases in muffin tins. Combine all the cupcake ingredients in a large bowl and beat with an electric whisk until smooth and pale, about 2 to 3 minutes. Spoon the batter into the cups. Bake for 20 minutes. Remove tins from the oven and cool for 5 minutes. Then remove the cupcakes and cool on a rack. For the florentine topping, combine all the ingredients except the chocolate in a small bowl. Spoon small teaspoons of the mixture onto greaseproof paper-lined baking trays. Bake for 5 minutes, until golden. Remove from the oven and cool for 1 minute. Remove the florentines from the sheet and crumble. Scatter over the cooled cupcakes and drizzle with the chocolate. Store in an airtight container for up to 2 days, or freeze for up to 3 months.

Makes 1¹/₂ dozen

strawberries 'n' cream cupcakes

see variations page 147

This recipe is great for lazy summer days when plump, sweet and juicy strawberries are at the height of their season.

for the cupcakes
225 g (8 oz) unsalted butter, softened
225 g (8 oz) caster sugar
225 g (8 oz) self-raising flour
4 eggs
1 tsp vanilla essence

for the topping
350 ml (12 fl oz) whipping cream
4 tbsp icing sugar, sieved
1 tsp vanilla essence
375 g (13 oz) sliced small strawberries
4 tbsp strawberry jelly
1 tbsp water

Preheat the oven to 175°C (350°F / Gas mark 4). Place 18 paper baking cases in muffin tins. Combine all the cupcake ingredients in a medium bowl and beat with an electric whisk until smooth and pale, about 2 to 3 minutes.

Spoon the batter into the cases. Bake for 20 minutes. Remove tins from the oven and cool for 5 minutes. Then remove the cupcakes and cool on a rack.

For the topping, whisk the cream, icing sugar and vanilla in a small bowl until soft peaks form. Spoon onto the cooled cupcakes and arrange the strawberries on top. In a small saucepan heat the jelly and water until melted. Brush the mixture on top of the strawberries. Chill until ready to serve. Store in an airtight container in the refrigerator for up to 2 days.

Makes 1^1/$_2$ dozen

baked cheesecakes

see variations page 148

These mouthwatering little cupcakes make stunning individual desserts. Make them ahead of time and all you'll have to do is pop them on a plate when your guests are ready.

125 g (4½ oz) digestive biscuit crumbs
5 tbsp unsalted butter, melted
450 g (1 lb) ricotta cheese
450 g (1 lb) cream cheese, softened

2 tsp vanilla essence
175 g (6 oz) icing sugar, sieved
3 eggs
150 g (5 oz) fresh blueberries

Preheat the oven to 160°C (325°F / Gas mark 3). Place 12 paper baking cases in a muffin tin.

Put the digestive biscuit crumbs into a medium bowl and stir in the butter. Spoon tablespoons of the crumb mixture into the cases, pressing firmly into the bottom. Chill until set.

In a large bowl, beat the ricotta until smooth. Add the cream cheese, vanilla and icing sugar, blending until smooth. Slowly add the eggs, blending well. Spoon the mixture into the cases.

Bake for 25 minutes. Remove tin from oven and cool for 5 minutes. Then remove the cupcakes and cool on a rack. Chill until time to serve. Serve topped with blueberries.

Store covered for up to 2 days in the refrigerator.

Makes 1 dozen

kahlua & orange cupcakes

see variations page 149

The combination of Kahlua and orange is wonderful. It makes a delightful drink, and a scrumptious cupcake, too!

for the cupcakes
225 g (8 oz) unsalted butter, softened
225 g (8 oz) caster sugar
225 g (8 oz) self-raising flour
4 eggs
1 tsp orange essence

for the icing
225 g (8 oz) icing sugar, sieved
115 g (4 oz) unsalted butter, softened
60 ml (2½ fl oz) soured cream
2 tbsp Kahlua
1 tbsp grated orange zest

Preheat the oven to 175°C (350°F / Gas mark 4). Place 18 paper baking cases in muffin tins. Combine all the cupcake ingredients in a medium bowl and beat with an electric whisk until smooth and pale, about 2 to 3 minutes. Spoon the batter into the cases. Bake for 20 minutes. Remove tins from the oven and cool for 5 minutes. Then remove the cupcakes and cool on a rack.

To make the icing, beat the icing sugar and butter in a small bowl until soft and creamy. Beat in the soured cream, Kahlua and orange zest. Swirl onto the cooled cupcakes.

Store without icing in an airtight container for up to 2 days, or freeze for up to 3 months.

Makes 1½ dozen

hot chocolate fondant cupcakes

see variations page 150

These cupcakes are very simple but must be served immediately. You can prepare the ramekins and batter in advance.

for the cupcakes
215 g (7½ oz) plain dark chocolate, broken into
  pieces
225 g (8 oz) unsalted butter, softened
4 eggs
4 egg yolks
115 g (4 oz) caster sugar
3 tbsp plain flour

for the topping
200 ml (7 fl oz) soured cream
Cocoa powder or icing sugar
  for dusting

Preheat the oven to 190°C (375°F / Gas mark 5). Butter 8 medium-sized ramekins. Dust each with flour, and tap out the excess. Melt the chocolate and butter in a medium bowl over a pan of simmering water. Stir until smooth. Set aside to cool. In a large bowl, beat the eggs, egg yolks and sugar until pale and creamy. Gradually add the melted chocolate, stirring until combined. Stir in the flour. Pour the batter into the ramekins and bake for 15 minutes, or until the tops are set.

Turn out onto serving plates. Top each with a dollop of soured cream, and dust with cocoa powder or icing sugar. Serve swiftly.

Makes 8

brioche bread pudding cupcakes

see variations page 151

Try this rich and robust cupcake recipe for an unusual and tasty twist on the classic bread and butter pudding.

for the custard
2 eggs
115 g (4 oz) caster sugar
1 tsp vanilla essence
450 ml (16 fl oz) whipping cream

for the cupcakes
12 thin slices brioche (crusts removed)
4 tbsp unsalted butter
90 g (3¼ oz) fresh raspberries

To make the custard, cream the eggs, sugar and vanilla in a small bowl. Add the cream, stir well and put aside. Preheat the oven to 175°C (350°F / Gas mark 4). Grease 12 small moulds with a little melted butter. Butter both sides of the bread and cut each slice into 12 small triangles. Push 3 triangles of bread into each mould, covering the bottom. Add a layer of raspberries. Pour a layer of custard over the raspberries. Repeat the process until there are four layers of each in each mould.

Place the moulds in a roasting tray. Pour boiling water into the tray until it reaches half way up the moulds. Bake until golden and firm, about 25 minutes. If the puddings begin to colour too much, cover the tray with kitchen foil.

Turn the puddings out of the moulds and serve warm. Store covered in the refrigerator for up to 2 days.

Makes 1 dozen

mini espresso cupcakes

see variations page 152

Making these cupcakes in espresso cups adds a special touch to the end of a meal.

for the cupcakes
175 g (6 oz) plain flour
1½ tsp baking powder
Pinch of salt
75 g (3 oz) malted milk powder
50 ml (2 fl oz) dark espresso coffee
115 g (4 oz) caster sugar
2 eggs
115 g (4 oz) unsalted butter, softened

for the icing
225 g (8 oz) unsalted butter, softened
340 g (11½ oz) icing sugar, sieved
1 tbsp instant coffee granules
2 tsp hot coffee
1 tsp vanilla essence

Preheat the oven to 175°C (350°F / Gas mark 4). Place 18 paper baking cases in espresso cups or mini muffin tins. Sieve the flour, baking powder and salt into a medium bowl. Combine the milk powder and coffee in a small bowl. Beat the sugar, eggs and butter in a medium bowl until light and creamy. Add the flour and coffee mixtures alternately to the egg mixture. Spoon the mixture into the prepared cups. Bake for 15 minutes. Remove cups from oven and cool for 5 minutes. Then remove the cupcakes and cool on a rack.

To make the icing, beat the butter and icing sugar in a bowl until soft and creamy. Add the coffee granules to the hot coffee and stir. Beat into the butter and sugar mixture, and then stir in the vanilla. Spread the icing onto the cooled cupcakes. Store unfrosted for up to 2 days in an airtight container, or freeze for up to 3 months.

Makes 1½ dozen

almond & raspberry friands

see variations page 153

Try using different oval or rectangular-shaped friand tins. They are available from speciality cookware shops.

190 g (6½ oz) unsalted butter, softened
100 g (3½ oz) ground almonds
6 egg whites
75 g (3 oz) plain flour

100 g (3½ oz) fresh raspberries
115 g (4 oz) caster sugar
Icing sugar for dusting

Preheat the oven to 175°C (350°F / Gas mark 4). Grease 12 small friand tins with a little of the butter. Mix all the ingredients in a large bowl, reserving half the raspberries, until just combined. Pour the batter into the prepared tins and scatter the remaining raspberries on top. Bake for 25 minutes, until golden and firm.

Remove tins from the oven and cool for 5 minutes. Turn friands out onto a rack and cool completely. Serve dusted with icing sugar.

Store in an airtight container for up to 2 days.

Makes 1 dozen

lime meringue cupcakes

see variations page 154

An unusual take on the classic lemon meringue pie. These cupcakes look and taste great!

for the cupcakes
225 g (8 oz) unsalted butter, softened
225 g (8 oz) caster sugar
225 g (8 oz) self-raising flour
4 eggs
1 tsp vanilla essence

for the filling
75 ml (3 fl oz) lime juice
400 g (14 oz) tin condensed milk

for the meringue
3 egg whites
¼ tsp cream of tartar
75 g (3 oz) granulated sugar

Preheat the oven to 175°C (350°F / Gas mark 4). Place 18 paper baking cases in muffin tins. Place all the cupcake ingredients in a large bowl and beat with an electric whisk until smooth and pale, about 2 to 3 minutes. Spoon the batter into the cases. Bake for 20 minutes. Remove tins from the oven and cool for 5 minutes. Then remove the cupcakes and cool on a rack. For the filling, combine the lime juice and condensed milk in a small bowl. Remove the top from each cupcake and hollow out a small hole. Spoon the filling into the hole and replace the top. For the meringue, beat the eggs and cream of tartar until soft peaks form. Add one-third of the sugar and beat for 1 minute. Repeat until all the sugar has been added. Increase the oven temperature to 230°C (450°F / Gas mark 8). Spoon or pipe the meringue on top of the cupcakes. Bake for 5 minutes until golden. Store for no more than 1 day in an airtight container.

Makes 1¹/₂ dozen

mocha & walnut cupcakes

see variations page 155

The coffee and walnuts set off the sweetness of these delicious cupcakes.

for the cupcakes
225 g (8 oz) unsalted butter, softened
225 g (8 oz) caster sugar
225 g (8 oz) self-raising flour
4 eggs
1 tsp vanilla essence
100 g (3½ oz) chopped walnuts

for the icing
225 g (8 oz) unsalted butter, softened
340 g (11½ oz) icing sugar, sieved
1 tbsp instant coffee granules
1 tsp hot coffee
1 tsp coffee liqueur
1 tsp vanilla essence

Preheat the oven to 175°C (350°F / Gas mark 4). Place 18 paper baking cases in muffin tins. Combine all the cupcake ingredients, except the walnuts, in a medium bowl and beat with an electric whisk until smooth and pale, about 2 to 3 minutes. Stir in the walnuts. Spoon the batter into the cases. Bake for 20 minutes. Remove tins from the oven and cool for 5 minutes. Then remove the cupcakes and cool on a rack.

For the icing, beat the butter and icing sugar in a bowl until soft and creamy. Combine the coffee granules and the hot coffee, then stir into the batter. Stir in the coffee liqueur and the vanilla. Spread the icing onto the cooled cupcakes.

Store without icing for up to 2 days in an airtight container, or freeze for up to 3 months.

Makes 1½ dozen

chocolate prune cupcakes

see variations page 156

The combination of dark chocolate and prunes makes this cupcake pure decadence.

for the cupcakes
225 g (8 oz) unsalted butter, softened
225 g (8 oz) caster sugar
225 g (8 oz) self-raising flour
4 eggs
1 tsp vanilla essence
100 g (3½ oz) plain dark chocolate chips
100 g (3½ oz) chopped dried prunes

for the icing
175 g (6 oz) icing sugar, sieved
115 g (4 oz) unsalted butter, softened
100 g (3½ oz) Dutch-process cocoa powder
2 tbsp chocolate liqueur
1 tsp vanilla essence

Preheat the oven to 175°C (350°F / Gas mark 4). Place 18 paper baking cases in muffin tins. Combine all the cupcake ingredients, except the chocolate chips and prunes, in a large bowl and beat with an electric whisk until smooth and pale, about 2 to 3 minutes. Stir in the prunes and chocolate. Spoon the batter into the cases. Bake for 20 minutes. Remove tins from the oven and cool for 5 minutes. Then remove the cupcakes and cool on a rack.

For the icing, beat the icing sugar and butter in a small bowl until creamy and smooth. Beat in the cocoa. Fold in the chocolate liqueur and vanilla. Spread the icing onto the cooled cupcakes.

Store without icing in an airtight container for up to 3 days, or freeze for up to 3 months.

Makes 1½ dozen

pineapple upside-down cupcakes

see variations page 157

A classic cake scaled down to a cupcake! When turning out the cupcakes, allow the sweet juices of the pineapple to be absorbed into the golden sponge.

for the topping
570 g (1 lb 4 oz) pineapple chunks
125 g (4½ oz) unsalted butter, melted
150 g (5 oz) brown sugar

for the cupcakes
225 g (8 oz) unsalted butter, softened
225 g (8 oz) caster sugar
225 g (8 oz) self-raising flour
4 eggs
1 tsp vanilla essence

Preheat the oven to 175°C (350°F / Gas mark 4). Grease two 12-cup muffin tins with butter and dust with a little flour, tapping out the excess. In the bottom of each cup, drizzle 1 tablespoon melted butter, 1 tablespoon pineapple and 1 tablespoon brown sugar.

Place all the cupcake ingredients in a large bowl and beat with an electric whisk until smooth and pale, about 2 to 3 minutes. Spoon the batter on top of the pineapple mixture in each cup. Bake for 25 minutes. Remove tins from the oven and cool for 10 minutes.

Turn out cupcakes onto dessert plates, serve warm with double cream if desired.

Store in an airtight container for up to 2 days.

Makes 2 dozen

little caramel cupcakes

see variations page 158

These delightful cupcakes contain a rich and gooey caramel surprise. They are an ideal companion for a cup of Earl Grey tea.

115 g (4 oz) unsalted butter, softened
150 g (5 oz) brown sugar
2 lightly beaten eggs
2 tbsp instant coffee granules

1 tbsp boiling water
300 g (10½ oz) self-raising flour
115 ml (4 fl oz) milk
125 g (4½ oz) soft caramels

Preheat the oven to 175°C (350°F / Gas mark 4). Place 12 paper baking cases in a muffin tin.

In a medium bowl, beat the butter and sugar until pale and creamy. Add the eggs slowly. In a small bowl, dissolve the coffee in the water. Beat the coffee into the butter mixture. Add the flour and milk, and beat until well combined.

Spoon the mixture into the cases. Push a couple of the caramels into the centre of each cupcake, and place them in the oven.

Bake for 20 minutes. Cool for 5 minutes in the tin. Turn onto a plate and serve while warm.

Store in an airtight container for up to 2 days.

Makes 1 dozen

sticky toffee pudding cupcakes

see variations page 159

This is an old classic British pudding that has recently enjoyed a bit of a renaissance.

for the cupcakes
175 g (6 oz) self-raising flour
100 g (3½ oz) brown sugar
115 g (4 fl oz) milk
1 egg
1 tsp vanilla essence
3 tbsp unsalted butter, melted
200 g (7 oz) chopped dates

for the topping
200 g (7 oz) brown sugar
2 tbsp unsalted butter
500 ml (16½ fl oz) boiling water

Preheat the oven to 190°C (375°F / Gas mark 5). Line 8 muffin cups in a tin with greaseproof paper. In a medium bowl, combine the flour and sugar. In a separate medium bowl beat the milk, eggs, vanilla and butter until smooth and pale, about 2 to 3 minutes. Pour the batter over the flour mixture and stir with a wooden spoon. Fold in the dates. Scrape the mixture into the muffin pans, filling each cup about halfway. For the topping, sprinkle 1 tablespoon of the sugar on top of the batter in each cup. Add ½ tablespoon butter, then pour about 1 tablespoon water over each.

Bake for 25 minutes. Remove from oven and cool for 5 minutes in the tin. Invert onto plates, peel off greaseproof paper and serve immediately.

Makes 8

variations

florentine cupcakes

see base recipe page 125

chocolate chip florentine cupcakes
Prepare the basic cupcake recipe, adding 100 g (3½ oz) plain chocolate chips after creaming the batter.

cherry florentine cupcakes
Prepare the basic cupcake recipe, adding 3 tablespoons chopped glacé cherries after creaming the batter.

almond florentine cupcakes
Prepare the basic cupcake recipe, adding 3 tablespoons chopped blanched almonds after creaming the batter.

strawberries 'n' cream cupcakes

see base recipe page 127

strawberries 'n' white chocolate cupcakes
Prepare the basic cupcake recipe, adding 100 g (3½ oz) white chocolate chips
to the creamed batter.

strawberries 'n' honey cupcakes
Prepare the basic cupcake recipe. For the topping, substitute 2 tablespoons
honey for the icing sugar.

strawberries 'n' lime cupcakes
Prepare the basic cupcake recipe. For the topping, substitute 1 tablespoon
lime juice for the vanilla essence. Substitute 4 tablespoons lime marmalade
for the strawberry jam.

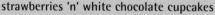

variations

baked cheesecakes

see base recipe page 128

banana & raisin baked cheesecakes
Prepare the basic cupcake recipe, adding 125 g (4½ oz) mashed banana (about 1 banana) to the cheese mixture before adding the eggs. Add 4 tablespoons raisins to the mixture after adding the eggs.

raspberry baked cheesecakes
Prepare the basic cupcake recipe, adding 100 g (3½ oz) fresh raspberries after mixing in the egg.

maple syrup baked cheesecakes
Prepare the basic cupcake recipe, substituting 90 g (3¼ oz) maple syrup for the icing sugar.

variations

kahlua & orange cupcakes

see base recipe page 130

white chocolate chip kahlua cupcakes
Prepare the basic cupcake recipe, adding 100 g (3½ oz) white chocolate chips
to the creamed batter.

dark chocolate chip kahlua cupcakes
Prepare the basic cupcake recipe, adding 100 g (3½ oz) plain dark chocolate
chips to the creamed batter.

raisin & brazil nut kahlua cupcakes
Prepare the basic cupcake recipe, adding 50 g (2 oz) raisins and 50 g (2 oz)
chopped Brazil nuts to the creamed batter.

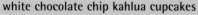

variations

hot chocolate fondant cupcakes

see base recipe page 131

strawberry cream fondant cupcakes
Prepare the basic cupcake recipe. Purée 5 medium-size, fresh strawberries in a food processor. Beat 225 ml (8 fl oz) whipping cream with 1 teaspoon vanilla essence until it is soft but holds its shape. Fold in the puréed strawberries. Spoon over the hot cupcakes.

orange cream fondant cupcakes
Prepare the basic cupcake recipe. Beat 225 ml (8 fl oz) whipping cream with 1 teaspoon orange essence and 2 tablespoons icing sugar until it is soft but holds its shape. Spoon liberally over the hot cupcakes.

crème chantilly fondant cupakes
Prepare the basic cupcake recipe. Beat 225 ml (8 fl oz) whipping cream with 1 teaspoon vanilla essence and 2 tablespoons icing sugar until it is soft but holds its shape. Spoon over the hot cupcakes.

brioche bread pudding cupcakes

see base recipe page 132

blueberry bread pudding cupcakes
Prepare the basic cupcake recipe, substituting 90 g (3¼ oz) fresh blueberries for the raspberries.

cherry bread pudding cupcakes
Prepare the basic cupcake recipe, substituting 90 g (3¼ oz) chopped glacé cherries for the raspberries.

chocolate chip bread pudding cupcakes
Prepare the basic cupcake recipe, substituting 90 g (3¼ oz) plain chocolate chips for the raspberries.

variations

mini espresso cupcakes

see base recipe page 134

mini chocolate espresso cupcakes
Prepare the basic cupcake recipe, adding 3 tablespoons plain chocolate chips after creaming the batter.

mini cinnamon espresso cupcakes
Prepare the basic cupcake recipe, sifting 2 teaspoons cinnamon into the dry ingredients.

mini espresso cupcakes with tia maria
Prepare the basic cupcake recipe, adding 2 tablespoons Tia Maria liqueur to the icing.

almond & raspberry friands

see base recipe page 135

strawberry friands
Prepare the basic cupcake recipe, substituting 100 g (3½ oz) fresh
strawberries for the raspberries.

chocolate & pecan friands
Prepare the basic cupcake recipe, substituting 3 tablespoons chopped
pecans and 3 tablespoons plain chocolate chips for the raspberries.

raisin friands
Prepare the basic cupcake recipe, substituting 100 g (3½ oz) raisins for
the raspberries.

variations

lime meringue cupcakes

see base recipe page 136

ice cream meringue cupcakes
Prepare the basic cupcake recipe, substituting 1 teaspoon ice cream for
the original filling. Pop the cupcakes in the freezer until ready to serve.

chocolate meringue cupcakes
Prepare the basic cupcake recipe. For the filling, substitute 100 g (3½ oz)
plain chocolate chips for the milk and lime juice. Melt the chocolate in a
medium bowl over a pan of simmering water and cool slightly. Spoon the
chocolate into the hole and refrigerate until set. Decorate with the meringue
when the chocolate has cooled. Bake for 5 minutes until meringue is golden.

lemon meringue cupcakes
Prepare the basic cupcake recipe. For the filling, substitute 75 ml (3 fl oz)
lemon juice for the key lime juice.

mocha & walnut cupcakes

see base recipe page 138

coffee, walnut & orange cupcakes
Prepare the basic cupcake recipe. For the icing, substitute 1 tablespoon grated orange zest for the vanilla essence.

irish cream & walnut cupcakes
Prepare the basic cupcake recipe. For the icing, substitute 2 tablespoons Irish Cream liqueur for the vanilla essence and coffee liqueur.

chocolate chip & walnut cupcakes
Prepare the basic cupcake recipe, adding 60 g (2½ oz) plain chocolate chips after creaming the cupcake batter.

variations

chocolate prune cupcakes

see base recipe page 139

orange, chocolate & prune cupcakes
Prepare the basic cupcake recipe, adding 1 tablespoon finely grated orange zest to the creamed batter.

walnut, chocolate & prune cupcakes
Prepare the basic cupcake recipe, adding 60 g (2½ oz) chopped walnuts after mixing in the chocolate chips and prunes.

hazelnut, chocolate & prune cupcakes
Prepare the basic cupcake recipe, adding 60 g (2½ oz) chopped toasted hazelnuts after mixing in the chocolate chips and prunes.

variations

pineapple upside-down cupcakes

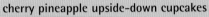

see base recipe page 140

cherry pineapple upside-down cupcakes
Prepare the basic cupcake recipe. Add 100 g (3½ oz) chopped cherries
to the pineapple mixture.

almond pineapple upside-down cupcakes
Prepare the basic cupcake recipe, adding 3 tablespoons chopped blanched
almonds to the creamed batter.

orange pineapple upside-down cupcakes
Prepare the basic cupcake recipe, adding 2 teaspoons orange essence
to the cupcake batter.

variations

little caramel cupcakes

see base recipe page 143

chocolate chip & caramel cupcakes
Prepare the basic cupcake recipe, mixing 4 tablespoons plain chocolate chips into the batter after the milk has been added.

ginger & caramel cupcakes
Prepare the basic cupcake recipe, mixing 3 tablespoons chopped crystallised ginger into the batter after the milk has been added.

chocolate nougat cupcakes
Prepare the basic cupcake recipe, substituting 6½ mini nougat bars for the caramel.

variations

sticky toffee pudding cupcakes

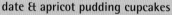

see base recipe page 144

date & apricot pudding cupcakes
Prepare the basic cupcake recipe. Substitute 200 g (7 oz) dried apricots
for half the chopped dates.

date & walnut pudding cupcakes
Prepare the basic cupcake recipe. Substitute 200 g (7 oz) chopped walnuts
for half the chopped dates.

date & pistachio pudding cupcakes
Prepare the basic cupcake recipe. Substitute 200 g (7 oz) chopped pistachios
for half the chopped dates.

muffins

Muffins are hearty and delicious. They can be served at any time of day – breakfast, brunch or lunch, tea or dinner. Muffins generally have fuller tops than cupcakes and are most likely to be served without any type of icing or topping.

blueberry muffins

see variations page 179

These classics are a great way to start the day. Serve them warm from the oven with a steaming cup of coffee or tea. If you can't get fresh blueberries, use frozen ones.

125 g (4½ oz) caster sugar
1 tbsp grated lemon zest
265 g (9½ oz) plain flour
1 tbsp baking powder
2 lightly beaten eggs

225 ml (8 fl oz) milk
115 g (4 oz) unsalted butter, melted
1 tsp vanilla essence
225 g (8 oz) fresh or thawed frozen blueberries

Preheat the oven to 200°C (400°F / Gas mark 6). Place 12 paper baking cases in a muffin tin.

In a medium bowl, stir the sugar, lemon zest, flour and baking powder with a spoon.

In a large bowl, beat the eggs, milk, butter and vanilla with an electric whisk until smooth, about 1 minute. Add the dry ingredients and stir until the blueberries are just combined. Spoon the batter into the cases.

Bake in the oven for 20 minutes. Remove tin from the oven and cool for 5 minutes. Serve muffins immediately.

Store in an airtight container for up to 2 days, or freeze for up to 3 months.

Makes 1 dozen

raspberry & coffee muffins

see variations page 180

The combination of fruit and nuts gives these muffins a wonderful texture.

2 tbsp boiling water
2 tbsp instant coffee granules
1 tbsp milk
110 g (3¾ oz) unsalted butter, melted
3 tbsp chopped hazelnuts
400 g (14 oz) self-raising flour

175 g (6 oz) caster sugar
1 tsp bicarbonate of soda
2 lightly beaten eggs
265 ml (9½ fl oz) buttermilk
225 g (8 oz) fresh raspberries

Preheat the oven to 200°C (400°F / Gas mark 6). Grease a 12-cup muffin tin.

In a small bowl or cup, pour 2 tablespoons boiling water over the instant coffee. Stir in the milk. Set aside to cool. In a medium bowl, mix the hazelnuts, flour, sugar and bicarbonate of soda with a spoon. In a large bowl, beat the eggs and buttermilk with an electric whisk until combined, about 2 to 3 minutes. Stir in the cooled coffee. Add the flour mixture to the buttermilk mixture, stirring until nearly combined. Gently fold in the raspberries. Spoon the batter into the prepared tin.

Bake for 20 minutes. Remove tin from the oven and cool for 5 minutes. Serve immediately.

Store in an airtight container for up to 2 days, or freeze for up to 3 months.

Makes 1 dozen

beetroot & chocolate muffins

see variations page 181

Do not be alarmed – these muffins are truly marvellous! Use fresh beetroots, with the skin on, not tinned.

500 g (1 lb 2 oz) trimmed fresh beetroots
250 g (9 oz) self-raising flour
2 tbsp Dutch-process cocoa powder
225 g (8 oz) caster sugar

1 tsp baking powder
2 eggs
75 ml (3 fl oz) vegetable oil
75 ml (3 fl oz) buttermilk

Steam the beetroot for 50 minutes, until tender. Drain and rinse under cold water. When cool enough to handle, gently peel away the skin with your fingertips. You may need to wear latex gloves to avoid staining your hands purple. Place the peeled beetroot in a food processor and blend until smooth. Set aside.

Preheat the oven to 175°C (350°F / Gas mark 4). Grease a 12-cup muffin tin. In a medium bowl, combine the flour, cocoa, sugar and baking powder. In a large bowl, beat the eggs, oil and buttermilk. Stir in the beetroot until well combined. Add the flour mixture, stirring until just combined. Spoon the batter in the prepared tin. Bake for 20 minutes. Remove tin from the oven and cool for 5 minutes. Then remove the muffins and cool on a rack.

Store in an airtight container for up to 2 days, or freeze for up to 3 months.

Makes 1 dozen

tomato & basil muffins

see variations page 182

Tomato and basil are a classic combination. Treat your basil kindly, and don't chop it too much.

2 tbsp chopped fresh basil	4 lightly beaten eggs
320g (11 oz) plain flour	125 ml (4½ fl oz) olive oil
2 tbsp baking powder	320 g (11 oz) tin condensed tomato soup
Pinch of salt	3 tbsp sun-dried tomatoes

Preheat the oven to 175°C (350°F / Gas mark 4). Grease a 12-cup muffin tin.

In a medium bowl, mix the basil, flour, baking powder and salt with a spoon.

In a large bowl, combine the eggs, olive oil, soup and sun-dried tomatoes with an electric whisk until well combined. Mix the flour mixture into the soup mixture until just combined. Spoon the mixture into the prepared tin. Bake for 20 minutes.

Remove tin from the oven and cool for 5 minutes. Remove the muffins and cool on a rack. Serve warm.

Store in an airtight container for up to 3 days, or freeze for up to 3 months.

Makes 1 dozen

apple & cinnamon muffins

see variations page 183

The apple and cinnamon complement each other without competing for attention.

320 g (11 oz) plain flour
250 g (9 oz) caster sugar
4 tsp baking powder
2 tsp cinnamon
4 tbsp vegetable oil

50 g (2 oz) unsalted butter, melted
2 lightly beaten eggs
175 ml (6 fl oz) buttermilk
2 peeled, cored and finely diced small apples

Preheat the oven to 175°C (350°F / Gas mark 4). Grease a 12-cup muffin tin.

In a medium bowl, combine the flour, sugar, baking powder and cinnamon. Set aside.

In a large bowl, beat the oil, butter, eggs and buttermilk with an electric whisk until well combined. Add the flour mixture and beat until nearly combined. Stir in the apples. Do not overmix. Spoon the mixture into the prepared tin.

Bake for 20 minutes Remove tin from the oven and cool for 5 minutes. Then remove the muffins and cool on a rack.

Store in an airtight container for up to 2 days, or freeze for up to 3 months.

Makes $^1/_2$ dozen

polenta muffins

see variations page 184

These splendid little muffins lend themselves to all manner of occasions. They work well with hearty dishes like chilli and pot roast.

265 g (9½ oz) self-raising flour
175 g (6 oz) polenta
60 g (2½ oz) caster sugar
1 tsp baking powder

Pinch of salt
250 ml (9 fl oz) buttermilk
100 g (3½ oz) unsalted butter, melted
1 lightly beaten egg

Preheat the oven to 175°C (350°F / Gas mark 4). Grease a large 6-cup muffin tin.

In a medium bowl, mix the flours, polenta, sugar, baking powder and salt with a spoon. Beat the buttermilk, butter and egg in a large bowl with an electric whisk. Stir the dry ingredients into the buttermilk mixture until just combined.

Spoon the batter into the prepared tin. Bake for 20 minutes.

Remove tin from the oven and cool for 5 minutes. Remove the muffins and cool on a rack. Serve warm.

Store in an airtight container for up to 2 days, or freeze for up to 3 months.

Makes ½ dozen

mixed berry crumble muffins

see variations page 185

These crumbly-topped muffins hide a sweet surprise. Serve them right out of the oven!

for the filling
275 g (10 oz) mixed berries (blackberries,
    strawberries, raspberries)
3 tbsp caster sugar
2 tbsp water
¼ tsp lemon zest

for the crumble
2 tbsp unsalted butter, melted
4 tbsp plain flour
3 tbsp light brown sugar

4 tbsp porridge oats
1 tsp lemon zest

for the muffins
375 g (13 oz) self-raising flour
125 g (4½ oz) brown sugar
Pinch of salt
1 tsp baking powder
115 g (4 oz) unsalted butter, melted
250 ml (9 fl oz) milk
1 egg

Preheat the oven to 200°C (400°F / Gas mark 6). Grease a 12-cup muffin tin. Combine all the filling ingredients in a small saucepan. Gently bring to a simmer and cook for 5 minutes, until the berries give some of their juices. Set aside. Stir all the crumble ingredients in a small bowl and set aside. For the muffins, combine the dry ingredients in a large bowl. In a medium bowl, beat the butter, milk and egg. Add the egg mixture to the dry ingredients and stir until just combined. Spoon a little batter into each cup, using about half the batter. Then spoon a layer of filling into the cups. Add the remaining batter and top with the crumble mixture. Bake for 20 minutes. Remove tin from the oven and cool for 5 minutes. Serve muffins warm. Store in an airtight container for up to 3 days, or freeze for up to 3 months.

Makes 1 dozen

rhubarb & pistachio muffins

see variations page 186

The pistachios and rhubarb give these muffins a wonderful colour.

for the filling
200 g (7 oz) chopped fresh rhubarb
4 tbsp caster sugar
2 tbsp water
1 tsp grated lemon zest

for the muffins
375 g (13 oz) plain flour
125 g (4½ oz) brown sugar
Pinch of salt
4 tsp baking powder
100 g (3½ oz) unsalted butter, melted
250 ml (9 fl oz) milk
1 lightly beaten egg
100 g (3½ oz) shelled pistachios

Preheat the oven to 200°C (400°F / Gas mark 6). Grease a 12-cup muffin tin. Combine all the filling ingredients in a saucepan over gentle heat. Bring slowly to a simmer and cook for 5 minutes, until the rhubarb is soft. Set aside. In a medium bowl, combine the flour, sugar, salt and baking powder. Mix well and set aside. In a large bowl, combine the butter, milk and egg with an electric whisk until combined. Stir in the flour mixture until nearly combined, then stir in the pistachios. Spoon a little mixture into the muffin cups, top with the cooled rhubarb and finally add the remaining muffin mixture. Bake for 20 minutes. Remove from the oven and cool for 5 minutes. Then remove the muffins and cool on a rack.

Store in an airtight container for up to 2 days, or freeze for up to 3 months.

Makes 1 dozen

peach & tomato muffins

see variations page 187

The marriage of peach and tomato may be unusual, but these muffins taste fantastic!

375 g (13 oz) self-raising flour
1 tsp baking powder
Pinch of salt
4 tbsp caster sugar
90 g (3¼ oz) unsalted butter, melted

1 lightly beaten egg
310 ml (10¾ fl oz) buttermilk
2 ripe medium peaches, sliced
3 tbsp chopped sun-dried tomatoes

Preheat the oven to 200°C (400°F / Gas mark 6). Grease a large 6-cup muffin tin.

In a medium bowl, mix the flour, baking powder, salt and sugar with a spoon.

In a large bowl, beat the butter, egg and buttermilk with an electric whisk. Add the flour mixture to the buttermilk mixture, stirring until nearly combined. Stir in the peaches and tomatoes.

Spoon the batter into the prepared tin. Bake for 20 minutes. Remove tin from the oven and cool for 5 minutes. Remove the muffins and cool on a rack.

Store refrigerated in an airtight container for up to 2 days, or freeze for up to 3 months.

Makes ¹/₂ dozen

smoked salmon &
black pepper muffins

see variations page 188

This muffin goes with any meal. Try serving it for brunch, slightly warm, with a soft-boiled egg.

225 g (8 oz) plain flour
1 tbsp baking powder
Pinch of salt
225 ml (8 fl oz) milk
2 lightly beaten eggs

3 tbsp unsalted butter, melted
100 g (3½ oz) finely chopped smoked salmon
1 tsp freshly ground black pepper
1 tbsp grated lemon zest

Preheat the oven to 175°C (350°F / Gas mark 4). Grease a large 6-cup muffin tin. In a medium bowl, combine the flour, baking powder and salt with a spoon.

In a large bowl, beat the milk, eggs and butter with an electric whisk. Add the salmon, black pepper and lemon zest. Gently fold the flour into the wet ingredients until just combined.

Spoon the mixture into the prepared tin. Bake for 20 minutes. Remove from the oven and cool for 5 minutes. Then remove the muffins and cool on a rack.

Store refrigerated in an airtight container for up to 2 days, or freeze for up to 3 months.

Makes ¹/₂ dozen

morning muesli muffins

see variations page 189

If you are usually in a hurry to get out the door in the morning, make a batch of these delicious and nutritious muffins the night before.

175 g (6 oz) finely chopped dried apricots
175 g (6 oz) dried muesli
250 g (9 oz) self-raising flour
1 tsp baking powder
125 ml (4½ fl oz) orange juice

125 ml (4½ fl oz) apple juice
3 tbsp vegetable oil
100 g (3½ oz) honey
1 lightly beaten egg

Preheat the oven to 175°C (350°F / Gas mark 4). Grease a 12-cup muffin tin. Mix the apricots, muesli, flour and baking powder in a medium bowl with a spoon. Set aside.

Beat the orange juice, apple juice, oil, honey and egg in a large bowl with an electric whisk. Add the flour mixture to the egg mixture and stir until just combined.

Spoon the mixture into the prepared tin. Bake for 20 minutes. Remove tin from the oven and cool for 5 minutes. Then remove the muffins and cool on a rack.

Store in an airtight container for up to 3 days, or freeze for up to 3 months.

Makes 1 dozen

caramelised onion muffins

see variations page 190

You can use any kind of onion in this recipe. You could try Vidalia onions, which have an incredible natural sweetness.

2 tbsp olive oil	1 tbsp baking powder
450 g (1 lb) finely sliced medium	Pinch of salt
Vidalia onions	2 lightly beaten eggs
1 tsp dried crushed chillies	190 g (6½ oz) unsalted butter, melted
450 g (1 lb) plain flour	320 ml (11 fl oz) buttermilk
350 g (12 oz) polenta	1 tbsp chopped fresh thyme leaves

Heat the oil in a medium frying pan. Add the onions and cook over medium heat, stirring occasionally until they are soft and caramelised, about 15 minutes. Set aside to cool.

Preheat the oven to 175°C (350°F / Gas mark 4). Grease a 12-cup muffin tin. In a medium bowl, mix the chillies, flour, polenta, baking powder and salt with a spoon. In a large bowl, beat the eggs, butter, buttermilk and thyme until combined. Stir in half the cooked onions. Stir in the flour mixture until just combined. Spoon the mixture into the prepared tin. Top with the remaining cooked onions. Bake for 20 minutes.

Remove tin from the oven and cool for 5 minutes. Then remove the muffins and serve warm.

Store in an airtight container for up to 2 days. Not suitable for freezing.

Makes 1 dozen

white chocolate &
macadamia nut muffins

see variations page 191

There can't be a more decadent combination than white chocolate and macadamia nuts!

300 g (10½ oz) self-raising flour
150 g (5 oz) caster sugar
200 g (7 oz) white chocolate chips
100 g (3½ oz) roughly chopped, lightly toasted
    macadamia nuts

Pinch of salt
4 tbsp butter, melted
175 ml (6 fl oz) buttermilk
1 lightly beaten egg

Preheat the oven to 175°C (350°F / Gas mark 4). Grease a large 6-cup muffin tin.

In a medium bowl, mix the flour, sugar, chocolate chips, nuts and salt with a spoon.

In a large bowl, beat the butter, buttermilk and egg with an electric whisk. Add the flour mixture to the buttermilk mixture, stirring until just combined. Do not overmix.

Spoon the mixture into the prepared tin. Bake for 25 minutes. Remove tin from the oven and cool for 5 minutes. Then remove the muffins and cool on a rack.

Store in an airtight container for up to 3 days, or freeze for up to 3 months.

Makes ½ dozen

variations

blueberry muffins

see base recipe page 161

strawberry muffins
Prepare the basic cupcake recipe, substituting 225 g (8 oz) quartered fresh strawberries for the blueberries.

raspberry muffins
Prepare the basic cupcake recipe, substituting 225 g (8 oz) fresh raspberries for the blueberries.

blackberry muffins
Prepare the basic cupcake recipe, substituting 225 g (8 oz) halved fresh blackberries for the blueberries.

variations

raspberry & coffee muffins

see base recipe page 163

raspberry & pine nut muffins
Prepare the basic muffin recipe, substituting 3 tablespoons whole pine nuts for the hazelnuts.

blueberry & coffee muffins
Prepare the basic muffin recipe, substituting 225 g (8 oz) fresh blueberries for the raspberries.

mixed berry & coffee muffins
Prepare the basic muffin recipe, substituting 115 g (4 oz) fresh blackberries for half the raspberries.

variations

beetroot & chocolate muffins

see base recipe page 164

beetroot, chocolate & orange muffins
Prepare the basic muffin recipe, adding 1 teaspoon orange essence to the batter before stirring in the beetroot.

beetroot & chocolate chip muffins
Prepare the basic muffin recipe, adding 3 tablespoons plain chocolate chips to the dry ingredients.

beetroot, chocolate & fennel muffins
Prepare the basic muffin recipe, adding 1 tablespoon crushed fennel seeds to the dry ingredients.

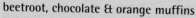

variations

tomato & basil muffins

see base recipe page 165

tomato, basil & mozzarella muffins
Prepare the basic muffin recipe, adding 100 g (3½ oz) grated mozzarella
cheese to the soup mixture.

tomato & marjoram muffins
Prepare the basic muffin recipe, substituting 2 tablespoons chopped fresh
marjoram for the basil.

tomato & chive muffins
Prepare the basic muffin recipe, substituting 2 tablespoons chopped fresh
chives for the basil.

apple & cinnamon muffins

see base recipe page 167

apple, cinnamon & walnut muffins
Prepare the basic muffin recipe, adding 100 g (3½ oz) chopped
walnuts along with the apples.

pear & cinnamon muffins
Prepare the basic muffin recipe, substituting 2 medium-sized pears
for the apples.

apple & spice muffins
Prepare the basic muffin recipe, adding ½ teaspoon ground cloves
to the dry ingredients.

variations

polenta muffins

see base recipe page 168

chilli & coriander polenta muffins
Prepare the basic muffin recipe, adding 1 teaspoon seeded and finely
chopped red chilli pepper and 3 tablespoons freshly chopped coriander
to the dry ingredients.

holy trinity polenta muffins
Prepare the basic muffin recipe, adding 3 tablespoons finely diced
red pepper, 2 tablespoons finely diced green pepper, and 2 tablespoons
finely chopped basil to the dry ingredients.

spicy sausage polenta muffins
Prepare the basic muffin recipe, adding 100 g (3½ oz) cooked
chopped Italian-style sausage.

mixed berry crumble muffins

see base recipe page 169

apple crumble muffins
Prepare the basic muffin recipe, substituting 320 g (11 oz) unsweetened apple sauce for the mixed berries.

peach crumble muffins
Prepare the basic muffin recipe, substituting 320 g (11 oz) tinned sliced peaches for the mixed berries.

rhubarb crumble muffins
Prepare the basic muffin recipe, substituting 320 g (11 oz) drained cooked rhubarb for the berries.

variations

rhubarb & pistachio muffins

see base recipe page 171

rhubarb & ginger muffins
Prepare the basic muffin recipe, substituting 3 tablespoons chopped crystallised ginger for the pistachios.

rhubarb & custard muffins
Prepare the basic muffin recipe. When the muffins have cooled, slice the top off each. Using a teaspoon, scoop out a small hole and fill with 1 teaspoon prepared custard. Replace the "lid".

rhubarb & orange flower muffins
Prepare the basic muffin recipe, adding 2 tablespoons orange flower water to the butter mixture.

peach & tomato muffins

see base recipe page 172

peach, tomato & lime muffins
Prepare the basic muffin recipe, adding 1 tablespoon freshly grated
lime zest to the buttermilk mixture.

peach, tomato & basil muffins
Prepare the basic muffin recipe, adding 2 tablespoons freshly chopped
basil to the buttermilk mixture.

peach, tomato & rosemary muffins
Prepare the basic muffin recipe, adding 1 teaspoon freshly chopped
rosemary to the buttermilk mixture.

smoked salmon & black pepper muffins

see base recipe page 174

smoked salmon & asparagus muffins
Prepare the basic muffin recipe, adding 200 g (7 oz) cooked chopped asparagus to the batter along with the salmon.

smoked salmon & mustard muffins
Prepare the basic muffin recipe, adding 2 tablespoons wholegrain mustard to the muffin batter along with the salmon.

smoked salmon & egg muffins
Prepare the basic muffin recipe. Place a whole soft-boiled egg in each muffin cup. Pour the muffin batter around and over it.

morning muesli muffins

see base recipe page 175

peach muesli muffins
Prepare the basic muffin recipe, substituting 175 g (6 oz) dried peaches
for the apricots.

coconut muesli muffins
Prepare the basic muffin recipe, adding 4 tablespoons desiccated coconut
to the dry ingredients.

maple muesli muffins
Prepare the basic muffin recipe, substituting 100 g (3½ oz) maple syrup for
the honey.

variations

caramelised onion muffins

see base recipe page 176

caramelised onion & rosemary muffins
Prepare the basic muffin recipe, substituting 1 tablespoon fresh rosemary for the thyme.

caramelised onion & gruyère muffins
Prepare the basic muffin recipe, adding 115 g (4 oz) grated Gruyère cheese to the batter before adding the onions.

caramelised two onion muffins
Prepare the basic muffin recipe, adding 3 tablespoons finely sliced green onions along with the other onions.

white chocolate & macadamia nut muffins

see base recipe page 178

white chocolate & date-nut muffins
Prepare the basic muffin recipe, adding 3 tablespoons chopped
dates to the mixture.

white chocolate & vanilla muffins
Prepare the basic muffin recipe, adding 1 teaspoon vanilla essence
to the buttermilk mixture.

white chocolate & pecan muffins
Prepare the basic muffin recipe, substituting 100 g (3½ oz) chopped
pecans for the macadamia nuts.

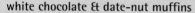

cupcakes for
special occasions

This chapter will provide inspiration for your next special occasion,

whether it is Valentine's Day, a birthday or a wedding.

st. patrick's day muffins

see variations page 212

These muffins are ideal to line the stomach before embarking on a day of toasting the Irish. Yes, they contain potatoes!

2 medium floury potatoes, peeled and cut
    into 6 mm (½ in) cubes
320 g (11 oz) plain flour
Pinch of salt
1 tbsp baking powder

1 lightly beaten egg
4 tbsp vegetable oil
250 ml (9 fl oz) buttermilk
3 tbsp chopped fresh chives
3 tbsp chopped fresh parsley

Preheat the oven to 175°C (350°F / Gas mark 4). Grease a 12-cup muffin tin with a little oil. In a small saucepan, cook the potatoes in boiling salted water for 8 minutes, or until just tender. Drain and rinse under cold water and set aside. In a medium bowl, combine the flour, salt and baking powder. In a large bowl, beat the egg, oil, buttermilk, chives and parsley. Stir the flour mixture into the buttermilk mixture until nearly combined. Gently fold in the potatoes.

Spoon the mixture into the prepared tin. Bake for 20 minutes. Remove tin from the oven and cool for 5 minutes. Then remove the muffins and cool on a rack. Serve with a glass of Guinness!

Store in an airtight container for up to 2 days, or freeze for up to 3 months.

Makes 1 dozen

easter egg nests

see variations page 213

These cute nests make the perfect gift for your little Easter bunnies.

for the cupcakes
225 g (8 oz) unsalted butter, softened
225 g (8 oz) caster sugar
225 g (8 oz) self-raising flour
4 eggs
1 tsp vanilla essence

for the icing
275 g (10 oz) chocolate, flaked
2 tbsp double cream
90 g (3¼ oz) chopped plain chocolate
54 miniature chocolate eggs

Preheat the oven to 175°C (350°F / Gas mark 4). Place 18 paper baking cases in muffin tins. Combine all the cupcake ingredients in a large bowl and beat with an electric whisk until smooth and pale, about 2 to 3 minutes. Spoon the batter into the cases.

Bake for 20 minutes. Remove tins from the oven and cool for 5 minutes. Then remove the cupcakes and cool on a rack.

To make the icing, put the chocolate and cream in a small saucepan over a low heat. Stir gently until combined. Remove from the heat and stir until the mixture is smooth. Swirl onto the cooled cupcakes. Top with shards of the chocolate and place 3 miniature eggs on top.

Store without icing in an airtight container for up to 3 days, or freeze for up to 3 months.

Makes 1¹/₂ dozen

wedding cupcakes

see variations page 214

These cupcakes are perfect for a home-style wedding. Each of your guests can take one home as a memento of the day.

for the cupcakes
225 g (8 oz) unsalted butter, softened
225 g (8 oz) caster sugar
225 g (8 oz) self-raising flour
4 eggs
1 tsp vanilla essence

for the icing
275 g (10 oz) icing sugar
2 tbsp lemon juice
54 sugared almonds
18 frosted roses

Preheat the oven to 175°C (350°F / Gas mark 4). Place 18 paper baking cases in muffin tins. Combine all the cupcake ingredients in a large bowl and beat with an electric whisk until smooth and pale, about 2 to 3 minutes.

Spoon the batter into the cases. Bake for 20 minutes. Remove tins from the oven and cool for 5 minutes. Then remove the cupcakes and cool on a rack.

To make the icing, sieve the icing sugar into a medium bowl. Add the lemon juice gradually, until it holds its shape. Spread onto the cupcakes, and top with almonds and roses.

Store in an airtight container for up to 3 days, or freeze without icing for up to 3 months.

Makes 1¹/₂ dozen

halloween pumpkin muffins

see variations page 215

Decorate these cupcakes with skeletons for when the trick-or-treaters come calling.

for the muffins
200 g (7 oz) plain flour
1 tsp cinnamon
1 tsp bicarbonate of soda
1 tsp baking powder
1 tsp mixed spice
265 g (9½ oz) caster sugar
115 ml (4 fl oz) vegetable oil

2 lightly beaten eggs
115 ml (4 fl oz) milk
150 g (5 oz) pumpkin purée

for the icing
50 g (2 oz) orange ready-rolled fondant icing
50 g (2 oz) black ready-rolled fondant icing
3 tbsp strawberry jam

Preheat the oven to 175°C (350°F / Gas mark 4). Place 6 large baking cases in a muffin tin. Dust two baking sheets with icing sugar. In a medium bowl, mix the dry ingredients. In a large bowl, beat the oil, eggs and milk. Stir in the pumpkin purée. Combine the flour mixture into the pumpkin mixture. Spoon into the cases. Bake for 20 minutes. Remove tin and cool for 5 minutes. Then remove the muffins and cool on a rack.

For the icing, roll the orange fondant to 3 mm (⅛ in) thick. Use a cutter or stencil to cut out Halloween shapes. Lay on one of the baking sheets. Roll the black fondant to 3 mm (⅛ in) thick. Cut 6 circles about 6 cm (2½ in) across. Set on the other baking sheet. Brush the top of each muffin with some jam. Lay the black fondant circles on top, followed by the orange Halloween shapes. Sprinkle with sweets. Store in an airtight container for up to 2 days.

Makes ½ dozen

passover cupcakes

see variations page 216

Make these with matzoh meal, also known as cake meal. We have added fresh
blueberries to these passover treats.

225 g (8 oz) caster sugar
115 ml (4 fl oz) vegetable oil
3 eggs
60 g (2½ oz) matzoh meal

2 tbsp potato starch
1 tsp ground cinnamon
225 g (8 oz) blueberries

Preheat the oven to 175°C (350°F / Gas mark 4). Place 12 paper baking cases in a 12-cup
muffin tin.

In a medium bowl, beat the sugar, oil and eggs with an electric whisk for 2 to 3 minutes.
Set aside. In a small bowl, sieve the matzoh meal, potato starch and cinnamon. Add the
dry ingredients to the egg mixture. Stir in the blueberries.

Spoon the mixture into the cases. Bake for 20 minutes.

Remove tin from the oven and cool for 5 minutes. Then remove the cupcakes and cool
on a rack. Store in an airtight container for up to 3 days, or freeze for up to 3 months.

Makes 1 dozen

irish barm brack cupcakes

see variations page 217

Traditionally, a coin and a ring are hidden in barm brack cakes. The person who finds the ring will soon be married and the person who finds the coin will soon be wealthy.

100 g (3½ oz) raisins
100 g (3½ oz) sultanas
100 g (3½ oz) currants
225 ml (8 fl oz) brewed black tea
450 g (1 lb) plain flour
1 tsp mixed spice

75 g (3 oz) brown sugar
1 tsp baking powder
Pinch of salt
1 egg
115 g (4 oz) unsalted butter, melted

In a large bowl, soak the dried fruits in the tea. Leave overnight or for a minimum of 6 hours.

Preheat the oven to 200°C (400°F / Gas mark 6). Grease a 12-hole muffin tin with a little oil. Mix the dry ingredients in a large bowl. In a separate large bowl, mix the egg and butter. Add the soaked and strained fruit, and stir well. Fold in the flour mixture.

Spoon the mixture into the prepared tin. (Optional: place a ring in one of the cakes and a coin in another.) Bake until the cupcakes are a dark golden colour and firm to the touch. Remove tin from the oven and cool for 5 minutes. Then remove the cupcakes and cool on a rack. Serve with unsalted butter. Store in an airtight container for up to 5 days, or freeze for up to 3 months.

Makes 1 dozen

king cupcakes

see variations page 218

Our version of the classic Mardi Gras "king cake." The colours traditionally used on the cake represent justice, faith and power.

for the cupcakes
225 g (8 oz) unsalted butter, softened
225 g (8 oz) caster sugar
225 g (8 oz) self-raising flour
4 eggs
1 tsp vanilla essence

for the icing
275 g (10 oz) icing sugar
2 tbsp lemon juice
2 tbsp gold-coloured sugar crystals
2 tbsp green-coloured sugar crysals
2 tbsp purple-coloured sugar crystals

Preheat the oven to 175°C (350°F / Gas mark 4). Place 18 paper baking cases in muffin tins. Combine all the cupcake ingredients in a large bowl and beat with an electric whisk until smooth and pale, about 2 to 3 minutes.

Spoon the batter into the cases. Bake for 20 minutes. Remove tins from the oven and cool for 5 minutes. Then remove the cupcakes and cool on a rack.

To make the icing, sieve the icing sugar in a medium bowl. Slowly add the lemon juice until the mixture becomes firm but spreadable. Spread onto the cupcakes, and sprinkle with the coloured sugar crystals.

Store in an airtight container for up to 3 days, or freeze without icing for up to 3 months.

Makes 1¹/₂ dozen

mini christmas tree cupcakes

see variations page 219

These fun and festive little cupcakes will look superb on your Christmas dessert table.

for the cupcakes
225 g (8 oz) unsalted butter, softened
225 g (8 oz) caster sugar
225 g (8 oz) self-raising flour
4 eggs
1 tsp vanilla essence

for the icing
175 g (6 oz) ready-rolled white fondant icing
175 g (6 oz) ready-rolled green fondant icing
2 tbsp raspberry jam
Coloured balls to decorate

Preheat the oven to 175°C (350°F / Gas mark 4). Place 18 mini paper baking cases in muffin tins. Dust two baking sheets with icing sugar. Combine all the cupcake ingredients into a large bowl and beat with an electric whisk until smooth and pale, about 2 to 3 minutes. Spoon the batter into the cases. Bake for 20 minutes. Remove tins from the oven and cool for 5 minutes. Then remove the cupcakes and cool on a rack. To make the icing, roll the white fondant to 3 mm ($^1/_8$ in) thick. Cut 18 circles using a 6-cm ($2^1/_2$-in) biscuit cutter and set them on one of the baking sheets. Roll the green fondant to 3 mm ($^1/_8$ in) thick. Using a small Christmas tree biscuit cutter, cut shapes out of the icing and place them on the other baking sheet to firm a little. Brush each cupcake with a little raspberry jam, then place a white fondant disc on top. Top with a Christmas tree and decorate with the coloured balls.

Store in an airtight container for up to 3 days, or freeze without icing for up to 3 months.

Makes 1$^1/_2$ dozen

christmas snowflake cupcakes

see variations page 220

These cupcakes are delightful for a Christmas gathering. You can serve them on
Christmas Eve when Santa's sleigh has set off and the kids are tucked into bed.

for the cupcakes
225 g (8 oz) unsalted butter, softened
225 g (8 oz) caster sugar
225 g (8 oz) self-raising flour
4 eggs
1 tsp vanilla essence

for the icing
115 g (4 oz) unsalted butter, softened
225 g (8 oz) icing sugar, sieved
1 tsp vanilla essence
2 tsp pale dry sherry
4 tbsp desiccated coconut

Preheat the oven to 175°C (350°F / Gas mark 4). Place 18 paper baking cases in muffin tins.
Combine all the cupcake ingredients in a large bowl and beat with an electric whisk until
smooth and pale, about 2 to 3 minutes.

Spoon the batter into the cases. Bake for 20 minutes. Remove tins from the oven and
cool for 5 minutes. Then remove the cupcakes and cool on a rack.

For the icing, beat the butter, icing sugar, vanilla and sherry in a medium bowl until
smooth and creamy. Spread on top of the cupcakes. Sprinkle a little coconut on top
to resemble snowflakes.

Store without icing in an airtight container for up to 3 days, or freeze for up to 3 months.

Makes 1 1/2 dozen

independence day cupcakes

see variations page 221

With their red, white and blue icing, these cupcakes make for a festive Fourth of July!

for the cupcakes
225 g (8 oz) unsalted butter, softened
225 g (8 oz) caster sugar
225 g (8 oz) self-raising flour
4 eggs
1 tsp vanilla essence

for the icing
115 g (4 oz) unsalted butter, softened
225 g (8 oz) icing sugar, sieved
1 tsp vanilla essence
200 g (7 oz) ready-rolled white fondant icing
175 g (6 oz) ready-rolled blue fondant icing
175 g (6 oz) ready-rolled red fondant icing

Preheat the oven to 175°C (350°F / Gas mark 4). Place 18 paper baking cases in muffin tins. Combine all the cupcake ingredients in a large bowl and beat with an electric whisk until pale and smooth, about 2 to 3 minutes. Spoon the batter into the cases. Bake for 20 minutes. Remove tins from the oven and cool for 5 minutes. Remove the cupcakes and cool on a rack.

To make the icing, beat the butter and icing sugar until soft and creamy. Add the vanilla and beat again. Spread onto the cooled cupcakes. Roll the white fondant to 3 mm ($^1/_8$ in) thick. Cut 18 circles using a 6-cm (2 $^1/_2$-in) biscuit cutter. Lay on top of the iced cupcakes. Roll the red fondant to 3 mm ($^1/_8$ in) thick. Cut small stars and lay on top of the white circles. Repeat for the blue fondant. Cut long 6-mm ($^1/_4$-in) strips of both red and blue to make stripes. If strips are too short, join them by lightly pressing with a rolling pin. Add to the circles and stars. Store without icing in an airtight container for up to 3 days.

Makes 1$^1/_2$ dozen

love-heart cupcakes

see variations page 222

These cupcakes make a delightful romantic gift for your true love on Valentine's Day – don't forget to attach a lover's message!

for the cupcakes
225 g (8 oz) unsalted butter, softened
225 g (8 oz) caster sugar
225 g (8 oz) self-raising flour
4 eggs
1 tsp vanilla essence

for the icing
175 g (6 oz) ready-rolled red fondant icing
175 g (6 oz) ready-rolled white fondant icing
3 tbsp raspberry jam
Silver balls

Preheat the oven to 175°C (350°F / Gas mark 4). Dust two baking sheets with icing sugar and put aside. Place 18 paper baking cases in muffin tins. Combine all the cupcake ingredients in a large bowl and beat with an electric whisk until smooth and pale, about 2 to 3 minutes. Spoon the batter into the cases. Bake for 20 minutes. Remove tins from the oven and cool for 5 minutes. Then remove cupcakes and cool on a rack.

To make the icing, roll the white fondant to 3 mm ($^1/_8$ in) thick. Cut 18 circles using a 6-cm ($2^1/_2$-in) biscuit cutter and set them on one of the baking sheets. Roll the red fondant to 3 mm ($^1/_8$ in) thick. Using a heart-shaped cutter, cut out 18 small hearts and set them on the other baking sheet. Brush each cupcake with a little jam and lay a white circle on top. Place a heart on top of the circle. Decorate with silver balls around the edge. Store in an airtight container for up to 3 days, or freeze without icing for up to 3 months.

Makes 1$^1/_2$ dozen

birthday cupcakes

see variations page 223

This is an easy and fun way to personalise birthday cupcakes!

for the cupcakes
225 g (8 oz) unsalted butter, softened
225 g (8 oz) caster sugar
225 g (8 oz) self-raising flour
4 eggs
1 tsp vanilla essence

for the icing
115 g (4 oz) unsalted butter, softened
225 g (8 oz) icing sugar, sieved
1 tsp vanilla essence
200 g (7 oz) ready-rolled white fondant icing
175 g (6 oz) ready-rolled blue fondant icing
175 g (6 oz) ready-rolled red fondant icing
Silver balls

Preheat the oven to 175°C (350°F / Gas mark 4). Place 18 paper baking cases in muffin tins. Combine all the cupcake ingredients in a large bowl and beat with an electric whisk until smooth and pale, about 2 to 3 minutes. Spoon the batter into the cases. Bake for 20 minutes. Remove tins from the oven and cool for 5 minutes. Then remove the cupcakes and cool on a rack. For the icing, beat the butter and icing sugar in a medium bowl until soft and creamy. Add the vanilla and beat again. Spread onto the cooled cupcakes. Roll the white fondant to 3 mm ($^1/_8$ in) thick. Cut 18 circles using a 6-cm ($2^1/_2$-in) biscuit cutter. Lay on top of the iced cupcakes. Roll the red and blue fondant to 3 mm ($^1/_8$ in) thick. Using miniature alphabet cutters, cut out initials and decorate the cupcakes. Garnish with silver balls.

Store without icing in an airtight container for up to 3 days, or freeze for up to 3 months.

Makes 1$^1/_2$ dozen

variations

st. patrick's day muffins

see base recipe page 193

spring onion muffins
Prepare the basic muffin recipe, adding 3 tablespoons sliced spring onions to the buttermilk mixture.

cabbage & caraway muffins
Prepare the basic muffin recipe, substituting 100 g (3½ oz) cooked cabbage and 1 teaspoon caraway seeds for the herbs.

bacon muffins
Prepare the basic muffin recipe, folding 3 tablespoons chopped, cooked bacon along with the potatoes.

variations

easter egg nests

see base recipe page 194

silver egg nests
Prepare the basic cupcake recipe, substituting 54 silver sugared almonds
for the miniature chocolate eggs.

orange-flavoured egg nests
Prepare the basic cupcake recipe, adding 1 teaspoon orange essence to
the chocolate icing.

chocolate chip egg nests
Prepare the basic cupcake recipe, folding 100 g (3½ oz) plain chocolate chips
to the creamed batter.

variations

wedding cupcakes

see base recipe page 197

primrose wedding cupcakes
Prepare the basic cupcake recipe, substituting 18 frosted primroses for the roses.

chocolate wedding cupcakes
Prepare the basic cupcake recipe, folding 100 g (3½ oz) plain chocolate chips into the creamed batter.

amaretto wedding cupcakes
Drizzle 3 tablespoons Amaretto over the cooled cupcakes before icing them.

variations

halloween pumpkin muffins

see base recipe page 198

raisin & pumpkin muffins
Prepare the basic muffin recipe, adding 100 g (3½ oz) raisins after folding
the flour mixture into the pumpkin mixture.

ginger & pumpkin muffins
Prepare the basic muffin recipe, adding 100 g (3½ oz) chopped crystallised
ginger after folding the flour mixture into the pumpkin mixture.

pecan & pumpkin muffins
Prepare the basic muffin recipe, adding 100 g (3½ oz) chopped pecans after
folding the flour mixture into the pumpkin mixture.

variations

passover cupcakes

see base recipe page 200

cranberry passover cupcakes
Prepare the basic cupcake recipe, substituting 225 g (8 oz) fresh cranberries for the blueberries.

orange & raisin passover cupcakes
Prepare the basic cupcake recipe, substituting 100 g (3½ oz) raisins for the blueberries. Add 1 teaspoon orange essence to the egg mixture.

lemon & ginger passover cupcakes
Prepare the basic cupcake recipe, substituting 1 tablespoon lemon zest and 3 tablespoons chopped crystallised ginger for the blueberries.

irish barm brack cupcakes

see base recipe page 201

sugar-glazed barm brack cupcakes
Prepare the basic cupcake recipe. Prepare a glaze by mixing 2 tablespoons boiling water with 1 tablespoon caster sugar. Brush the glaze on the cupcakes while they are still warm in the tin. Return the tin to the oven for a few minutes to allow the glaze to set and turn a shiny brown.

whiskey-glazed barm brack cupcakes
Prepare the basic cupcake recipe. Prepare a glaze by mixing 2 tablespoons warm Irish Whiskey with 1 tablespoon caster sugar. Brush the glaze on the cupcakes while they are still warm in the tin. Return the tin to the oven for a few minutes to allow the glaze to set and turn a shiny brown.

apricot barm brack cupcakes
Prepare the basic cupcake recipe, adding 100 g (3½ oz) chopped dried apricots to the dried fruit mixture. Increase quantity of black tea to 300 ml (10 fl oz).

variations

king cupcakes

see base recipe page 203

sultana king cupcakes
Prepare the basic cupcake recipe, folding 100 g (3½ oz) sultanas into
the creamed batter.

walnut king cupcakes
Prepare the basic cupcake recipe, folding 100 g (3½ oz) chopped walnuts
into the creamed batter.

white chocolate king cupcakes
Prepare the basic cupcake recipe, folding 100 g (3½ oz) white chocolate
chips into the creamed batter.

mini christmas tree cupcakes

see base recipe page 204

ginger & raisin christmas tree cupcakes
Prepare the basic cupcake recipe, adding 2 teaspoons ground ginger
to the cupcake ingredients, and folding 100 g (3½ oz) raisins into the
creamed batter.

orange & lemon christmas tree cupcakes
Prepare the basic cupcake recipe, adding 1 tablespoon grated orange zest
and 1 tablespoon grated lemon zest to the creamed batter.

white chocolate christmas tree cupcakes
Prepare the basic cupcake recipe, folding 100 g (3½ oz) white chocolate
chips into the creamed batter.

variations

christmas snowflake cupcakes

see base recipe page 206

poppy seed snowflake cupcakes
Prepare the basic cupcake recipe, adding 2 tablespoons poppy seeds
to the creamed batter.

mixed berry snowflake cupcakes
Prepare the basic cupcake recipe, folding 4 tablespoons dried mixed
cranberries, cherries and blueberries into the creamed batter.

hazelnut snowflake cupcakes
Prepare the basic cupcake recipe, folding 3 tablespoons roasted chopped
hazelnuts into the creamed batter.

independence day cupcakes

see base recipe page 207

raisin independence day cupcakes
Prepare the basic cupcake recipe, folding 100 g (3½ oz) raisins into the creamed batter.

white chocolate independence day cupcakes
Prepare the basic cupcake recipe, folding 100 g (3½ oz) white chocolate chips into the creamed batter.

crystallised peel independence day cupcakes
Prepare the basic cupcake recipe, folding 2 tablespoons chopped crystallised peel into the creamed batter.

variations

love-heart cupcakes

see base recipe page 208

white chocolate heart cupcakes
Prepare the basic cupcake recipe, folding 100 g (3½ oz) white chocolate chips into the creamed batter.

macadamia nut heart cupcakes
Prepare the basic cupcake recipe folding 100 g (3½ oz) lightly toasted and chopped macadamia nuts into the creamed batter.

cherry heart cupcakes
Prepare the basic cupcake recipe folding 4 tablespoons chopped glacé cherries into the creamed batter.

variations

birthday cupcakes

see base recipe page 211

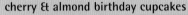

cherry & almond birthday cupcakes
Prepare the basic cupcake recipe, folding 2 tablespoons chopped
glacé cherries and 2 tablespoons chopped blanched almonds into
the creamed batter.

orange birthday cupcakes
Prepare the basic cupcake recipe, adding 1 teaspoon orange essence
to the creamed batter.

crystallised fruit birthday cupcakes
Prepare the basic cupcake recipe, folding 3 tablespoons chopped
crystallised citrus fruits into the creamed batter.

cupcakes for kids

Crisp rice cupcakes and mini peanut butter cupcakes are a great way to get kids involved in the kitchen. These cupcakes are so much fun to decorate, it can be a party in itself!

s'more cupcakes

see variations page 247

Building s'more cupcakes is great fun for everyone. They require little fuss and effort, with a quick assembly and baking time.

24 digestive biscuits
200 g (7 oz) chocolate bars, broken into
    12 squares

100 g (3½ oz) chopped walnuts
3 tbsp desiccated coconut
60 g (2½ oz) miniature marshmallows

Preheat the oven to 160°C (325°F / Gas mark 3). Place 12 paper baking cases in a muffin tin.

Lay a biscuit in the bottom of each case. Add a piece of chocolate, followed by a sprinkle of walnuts and coconut. Lay another biscuit on top.

Bake for 7 minutes, until the chocolate has melted. Remove tin from the oven and cool slightly. Push the biscuit "lids" down so that they are secure.

Pop a couple of marshmallows on top of each cupcake. Return tin to the oven for 10 minutes, until the marshmallows melt and brown slightly. Remove tin from the oven and cool for 5 minutes. Then remove the cupcakes and cool on a rack.

Store in an airtight container for up to 24 hours.

Makes 1 dozen

toadstool cupcakes

see variations page 248

These funky toadstool cupcakes will brighten up any children's party.

for the cupcakes
225 g (8 oz) unsalted butter, softened
225 g (8 oz) caster sugar
225 g (8 oz) self-raising flour
1 tsp baking powder
4 eggs
1 tsp vanilla essence

for the icing
375 g (13 oz) icing sugar, sieved
225 g (8 oz) unsalted butter, softened
Pinch of salt
Red food colouring
50 g (2 oz) ready-rolled white fondant icing

Preheat the oven to 175°C (350°F / Gas mark 4). Place 18 paper baking cases in muffin tins. Combine all the cupcake ingredients in a large bowl and beat with an electric whisk until smooth and pale, about 2 to 3 minutes. Spoon the batter into the cases. Bake for 20 minutes. Remove tins from the oven and cool for 5 minutes. Remove the cupcakes and cool on a rack.

To make the icing, cream the icing sugar, butter and salt in a medium bowl with an electric whisk until smooth. Add a few drops of the food colouring, and mix until the icing is a uniform bright red. Cut small circles out of the fondant icing. Spoon the red icing onto the cupcakes and place the white fondant circles on top.

Store without icing in an airtight container for up to 3 days, or freeze for up to 3 months.

Makes 1 1/2 dozen

ice cream cone cupcakes

see variations page 249

These cupcakes look like ice cream – but they won't melt!

for the cupcakes
225 g (8 oz) unsalted butter, softened
225 g (8 oz) caster sugar
225 g (8 oz) self-raising flour
1 tsp baking powder
4 eggs
1 tsp vanilla essence
24 mini flat-bottomed wafer cups

for the icing
175 g (6 oz) icing sugar, sieved
115 g (4 oz) unsalted butter, softened
Pinch of salt
115 ml (4 fl oz) whipping cream
1 tsp vanilla essence
2 tbsp coloured sprinkles

Preheat the oven to 175°C (350°F / Gas mark 4). Line a 24-cup mini muffin tin with paper baking cases. Combine all the cupcake ingredients in a large bowl and beat with an electric whisk until smooth and pale, about 2 to 3 minutes. Spoon the batter into the cases.

Bake for 20 minutes. Remove tin from the oven and cool for 5 minutes. Then remove the cupcakes and cool on a rack. Peel off the paper baking cases and place the cupcakes inside the ice cream cones. To make the icing, beat the sugar, butter, and salt using an electric whisk. Add the cream and vanilla, and beat until smooth. Pipe the mixture in a swirl on top of the cupcake. Shake some sprinkles on top.

Store without icing in an airtight container for up to 2 days.

Makes 2 dozen

think pink cupcakes

see variations page 250

Think pink while you're icing and you will have a whole manner of coloured cupcakes!

for the cupcakes
225 g (8 oz) unsalted butter, softened
225 g (8 oz) caster sugar
225 g (8 oz) self-raising flour
1 tsp baking powder
4 eggs
1 tsp vanilla essence

for the icing
375 g (13 oz) icing sugar, sieved
225 g (8 oz) unsalted butter, softened
Pinch of salt
Pink food colouring
Silver balls

Preheat the oven to 175°C (350°F / Gas mark 4). Place 18 paper baking cases in muffin tins. Combine all the cupcake ingredients in a large bowl and beat with an electric whisk until smooth and pale, about 2 to 3 minutes.

Spoon the batter into the cases. Bake for 20 minutes. Remove tins from the oven and cool for 5 minutes. Then remove the cupcakes and cool on a rack.

To make the icing, cream the icing sugar, butter and salt with an electric whisk until smooth. Add a few drops of food colouring, and mix well. Spread the icing liberally onto the cooled cupcakes and sprinkle with silver balls.

Store without icing in an airtight container for up to 3 days, or freeze for up to 3 months.

Makes 1¹/₂ dozen

cookies & cream cupcakes

see variations page 251

Mix crushed cookies into the batter to give a crispy crunch to these cupcakes.

for the cupcakes
225 g (8 oz) unsalted butter, softened
225 g (8 oz) caster sugar
225 g (8 oz) self-raising flour
1 tsp baking powder
4 eggs
1 tsp vanilla essence
10 crushed cream-filled chocolate cookies

for the icing
375 g (13 oz) icing sugar, sieved
225 g (8 oz) unsalted butter, softened
Pinch of salt
10 chopped cream-filled chocolate cookies

Preheat the oven to 175°C (350°F / Gas mark 4). Place 18 foil or paper baking cases in muffin tins. Combine all the cupcake ingredients, except the cookies, in a large bowl and beat with an electric whisk until smooth and pale, about 2 to 3 minutes. Stir in the cookies.

Spoon the batter into the cases. Bake for 20 minutes. Remove tins from the oven and cool for 5 minutes. Then remove the cupcakes and cool on a wire rack.

To make the icing, beat the icing sugar, butter and salt using an electric whisk. Spread the icing onto the cooled cupcakes and sprinkle the chopped cookies on top.

Store without icing in an airtight container for up to 3 days, or freeze for up to 3 months.

Makes 1¹/₂ dozen

alphabet cupcakes

see variations page 252

Line these up to spell somebody's name at a birthday party!

for the cupcakes
225 g (8 oz) unsalted butter, softened
225 g (8 oz) caster sugar
225 g (8 oz) self-raising flour
1 tsp baking powder
4 eggs
1 tsp vanilla essence

for the icing
175 g (6 oz) ready-rolled white fondant icing
3 tbsp raspberry jam
50 g (2 oz) ready-rolled red, green and black
    fondant icing
Coloured sprinkles

Preheat the oven to 175°C (350°F / Gas mark 4). Place 18 paper baking cases in muffin tins. Combine all the cupcake ingredients in a large bowl and beat with an electric whisk until smooth and pale, about 2 to 3 minutes. Spoon the batter into the cases. Bake for 20 minutes. Remove tins from the oven and cool for 5 minutes. Then remove the cupcakes and cool on a rack. For the icing, roll out the white fondant and cut 18 discs using a 5-cm (2-in) biscuit cutter. Brush the cupcakes with a little of the jam. Press the circles onto the cupcakes. Using mini alphabet cutters, cut letter shapes from the coloured fondant icing and place them on top of the white circles. Sprinkle the edges with coloured sprinkles.

Store without icing in an airtight container for up to 3 days, or freeze for up to 3 months.

Makes 1¹/₂ dozen

pineapple cupcakes

see variations page 253

These cupcakes melt in the mouth and are the perfect teatime treat. Serve with a cup of Earl Grey tea.

for the cupcakes
225 g (8 oz) unsalted butter, softened
225 g (8 oz) caster sugar
225 g (8 oz) self-raising flour
1 tsp baking powder
4 eggs
1 tsp vanilla essence
175 g (6 oz) drained crushed pineapple

for the icing
200 g (7 oz) cream cheese, softened
175 g (6 oz) icing sugar, sieved
1 tbsp lemon juice
1 tsp vanilla essence
50 g (2 oz) chopped walnuts

Preheat the oven to 175°C (350°F / Gas mark 4). Place 18 paper baking cases in muffin tins. Combine all the cupcake ingredients, except the pineapple, in a large bowl and beat with an electric whisk for about 2 to 3 minutes. Stir in the pineapple. Spoon the batter into the cases. Bake for 20 minutes. Remove tins from the oven and cool for 5 minutes. Then remove the cupcakes and cool on a rack. To make the icing, slowly beat the cream cheese and icing sugar in a large bowl with an electric whisk until creamy and soft. Add the lemon juice and vanilla, and beat briskly until well combined. Spread the icing onto the cooled cupcakes and garnish with the chopped walnuts.

Store without icing in an airtight container for 2 to 3 days, or freeze for up to 3 months.

Makes 1 1/2 dozen

mini peanut butter cupcakes

see variations page 254

Simple and no fuss. You can make these cupcakes in large batches, which makes them ideal for kids' parties and picnics.

375 g (13 oz) milk chocolate
2 tbsp unsalted butter
3 tbsp double cream
175 g (6 oz) smooth peanut butter

Place 12 mini foil baking cases in a muffin tin.

Place the chocolate, butter and cream in a medium bowl over a pan of simmering water, and stir until smooth. Remove from the heat and set aside.

With damp hands, shape the peanut butter into 12 small flat circles. Push the peanut butter into the bottom of the cases.

Pour the melted chocolate over the peanut butter, and refrigerate for at least 2 hours.

Store in an airtight container for up to 3 days.

Makes 1 dozen

crisp rice cupcakes

see variations page 255

I'm not too sure how many will reach the table, but these simple no-bake cupcakes are great fun for the budding young chef to try.

200 g (7 oz) dark chocolate
100 g (2½ oz) unsalted butter, softened
5 tbsp golden syrup
100 g (3½ oz) crisp rice cereal

Place 12 foil or paper baking cases on a tray.

Place the chocolate and butter in a medium bowl over a pan of simmering water, and stir until melted.

Remove tin from the heat and stir in the cereal and golden syrup.

Drop spoonfuls of the mixture into the cases. Refrigerate for 1 hour.

Store in an airtight container for up to 5 days.

Makes 1 dozen

eggy cupcakes

see variations page 256

Don't worry – you won't have to crack whole eggs to get this lovely sunny-side-up look.
Serve these cupcakes for breakfast with a glass of freshly squeezed juice.

for the cupcakes
225 g (8 oz) unsalted butter, softened
225 g (8 oz) caster sugar
225 g (8 oz) self-raising flour
1 tsp baking powder
4 eggs
1 tsp vanilla essence

for the icing
375 g (13 oz) icing sugar, sieved
225 g (8 oz) unsalted butter, softened
Pinch of salt
18 drained tinned peach halves

Preheat the oven to 175°C (350°F / Gas mark 4). Place 18 paper baking cases in muffin tins.
Combine all the cupcake ingredients in a large bowl and beat with an electric whisk until
smooth and pale, about 2 to 3 minutes. Spoon the batter into the cases. Bake for 20 minutes.
Remove tins from the oven and cool for 5 minutes. Remove the cupcakes and cool on a rack.

To make the icing, put the icing sugar, butter and salt in a large bowl and beat with an
electric whisk until smooth. Liberally spread the icing onto the cooled cupcakes and garnish
each cupcake with a peach half.

Store without icing in an airtight container for up to 3 days, or freeze for up to 3 months.

Makes 1¹/₂ dozen

chocolate berry cupcakes

see variations page 257

My good friend Beverley Glock gave me this recipe. She runs a company called "Splat," which organises children's parties where both children and adults can bake.

for the cupcakes
100 g (3½ oz) blackberries, fresh or thawed
    frozen
3 tbsp water
225 g (8 oz) caster sugar
100 g (3½ oz) self-raising flour
1 tsp baking powder

100 g (3½ oz) soft margarine
2 eggs
1 tbsp Dutch-process cocoa powder

for the ganache
150 g (5 oz) plain dark chocolate, broken
150 g (5 oz) double cream
12 blackberries

Preheat the oven to 175°C (350°F / Gas mark 4). Place 12 mini paper baking cases in a muffin tin. Place the blackberries, water and 115 g (4 oz) sugar in a small saucepan over low heat. Simmer for about 5 minutes, until the fruit starts to release its juices. Set aside to cool. Combine the rest of the ingredients in a medium bowl and beat with an electric whisk until pale and creamy, about 2 to 3 minutes. Spoon the batter into the cases. Spoon a little of the fruit on top. Bake for 20 minutes. Remove the tin and cool for 5 minutes. Then remove the cupcakes and cool on a rack. To make the ganache, melt the chocolate and cream in a medium bowl over a pan of simmering water, until glossy and smooth. Dollop a spoonful of ganache onto each cooled cupcake, and top with a blackberry. Refrigerate until set.

Store without ganache in an airtight container for up to 2 days, or freeze for up to 3 months.

Makes 1 dozen small cupcakes

space dust cupcakes

see variations page 258

Try these for a kid's party and watch their faces as the Space Dust explodes!

for the cupcakes
225 g (8 oz) unsalted butter, softened
225 g (8 oz) caster sugar
225 g (8 oz) self-raising flour
1 tsp baking powder
4 eggs
1 tsp vanilla essence

for the icing
115 g (4 oz) unsalted butter, softened
225 g (8 oz) icing sugar, sieved
1 tsp vanilla essence
2 sachets fruit-flavoured Space Dust

Preheat the oven to 175°C (350°F / Gas mark 4). Place 18 paper baking cases in muffin tins.

Combine all cupcake ingredients in a large bowl and beat with an electric whisk until smooth and pale, about 2 to 3 minutes. Spoon the batter into the cases.

Bake for 20 minutes. Remove tins from the oven and cool for 5 minutes. Then remove the cupcakes and cool on a rack.

To make the icing, cream the butter, icing sugar and vanilla in a medium bowl until smooth. Smear onto the cupcakes and sprinkle with Space Dust.

Store without icing in an airtight container for up to 2 days, or freeze for up to 3 months.

Makes 1 1/2 dozen

jam doughnut cupcakes

see variations page 259

These cupcakes aren't doughnuts, but I'm sure you'll see the likeness when you try one.

for the cupcakes
225 g (8 oz) unsalted butter, softened
225 g (8 oz) caster sugar
225 g (8 oz) self-raising flour
1 tsp baking powder
4 eggs
1 tsp vanilla essence
150 g (5 oz) raspberry jam

for the icing
200 g (7 oz) cream cheese, softened
175 g (6 oz) icing sugar, sieved
1 tbsp lemon juice
1 tsp of vanilla essence

Preheat the oven to 175°C (350°F / Gas mark 4). Place 18 paper baking cases in muffin tins. Combine all the cupcake ingredients, except the jam, in a large bowl and beat with an electric whisk, about 2 to 3 minutes. Spoon the batter into the cases. Bake for 20 minutes.

Remove tins from the oven and cool for 5 minutes. Then remove the cupcakes and cool on a rack. Slice the top off each cupcake, hollow out a small hole with a teaspoon and fill with the jam. Replace the top. To make the icing, slowly beat the cream cheese and icing sugar in a large bowl with an electric whisk until creamy and soft. Add the lemon juice and vanilla, and beat briskly until well combined. Spread the icing onto the cupcakes.

Store without icing in an airtight container for up to 2 days, or freeze for up to 3 months.

Makes 1¹/₂ dozen

variations

s'more cupcakes

see base recipe page 225

pecan s'more cupcakes
Prepare the basic cupcake recipe, substituting 100 g (3½ oz) roughly chopped pecans for the walnuts.

white chocolate s'more cupcakes
Prepare the basic cupcake recipe, substituting 50 g (2 oz) white chocolate chips for half the dark chocolate.

chocolate & raspberry s'more cupcakes
Prepare the basic cupcake recipe. Add 100 g (3½ oz) lightly crushed raspberries along with the coconut and walnuts.

variations

toadstool cupcakes

see base recipe page 227

koala bear cupcakes
Prepare the basic cupcake recipe. Omit the ready-rolled fondant. Colour the icing with brown food colouring instead of red. Make a koala face on each cupcake: a chocolate-covered brazil nut for the nose, 2 walnut halves for ears, and 2 sweets for the eyes.

sneaky snake cupcakes
Prepare the basic cupcake recipe. For the icing, substitute 50 g (2 oz) green ready-rolled fondant for the white fondant. Brush each cupcake with a little fruit jam. Roll the green fondant thinly and, using a biscuit cutter, cut 18 circles 6 cm (2¹/₂ in) across and place one on each cupcake. For the trees, cut 6 chocolate sticks into 3 sections 5 cm (2 in) in length, and stand upright on the fondant icing. Roll 50 g (2 oz) red fondant icing into 18 sausages 15 cm (6 in) in length. Curl the fondant around the chocolate "trees" and decorate with 2 sweets for the eyes.

bling bling cupcakes
Prepare the basic cupcake recipe. Omit the ready-rolled fondant. Decorate the red icing with silver and gold balls.

ice cream cone cupcakes

see base recipe page 228

chocolate-iced cone cupcakes
Prepare the basic cupcake recipe. To the icing, add 100 g (3½ oz) chocolate chips along with the cream and vanilla.

choc & mint-iced cone cupcakes
Prepare the basic cupcake recipe. To the icing, add 100 g (3½ oz) mint chocolate chips along with the cream. Substitute 1 teaspoon mint essence for the vanilla.

honey & cream-iced cone cupcakes
Prepare the basic cupcake recipe. To the icing, add 75 g (3 oz) honey after creaming the sugar and butter.

variations

think pink cupcakes

see base recipe page 231

azure cupcakes

Prepare the basic cupcake recipe. For the icing substitute blue food colouring for pink, and top with blue azure sugar crystals.

lavender sugar cupcakes

Prepare the basic cupcake recipe. For the icing substitute blue food colouring for pink. Make lavender sugar by combining 3 tablespoons lavender flowers and 175 g (6 oz) caster sugar in a food processor for about 2 minutes. Put the sugar in a cool dry place, and let the flavours mingle for about 2 hours. Sprinkle on top of the icing.

rose sugar cupcakes

Prepare the basic cupcake recipe. Make rose-petal sugar by combining 3 tablespoons red rose petals and 175 g (6 oz) caster sugar in a food processor for about 2 minutes. Put the sugar in a cool dry place, and let the flavours mingle for about 2 hours. Sprinkle on top of the icing.

cookies & cream cupcakes

see base recipe page 232

minted cookies & cream cupcakes
Prepare the basic cupcake recipe, using cream-filled mint chocolate cookies in both the cupcakes and the icing.

digestive biscuits & cream cupcakes
Prepare the basic cupcake recipe, substituting 90 g (3¼ oz) crushed digestive biscuits for 10 cookies in the cupcakes, and another 90 g (3¼ oz) crushed digestive biscuits for the cookies in the icing.

chocolate, nougat & cream cupcakes
Prepare the basic cupcake recipe, substituting 90 g (3¼ oz) chopped chocolate nougat bars for 10 cookies in the cupcakes, and another 90 g (3¼ oz) chopped nougat bars for the cookies in the icing.

alphabet cupcakes

see base recipe page 234

white chocolate alphabet cupcakes
Prepare the basic cupcake recipe, adding 100 g (3½ oz) white chocolate chips to the creamed batter.

raisin alphabet cupcakes
Prepare the basic cupcake recipe, adding 100 g (3½ oz) raisins to the creamed batter.

number cupcakes
Prepare the basic cupcake recipe. Use miniature number cutters instead of alphabet cutters.

pineapple cupcakes

see base recipe page 235

kicked-up chilli pineapple cupcakes
Prepare the basic cupcake recipe. Add 1 teaspoon seeded and finely chopped chilli pepper to the creamed batter.

orange & pineapple cupcakes
Prepare the basic cupcake recipe. Add 2 tablespoons orange zest to the creamed batter.

coconut & pineapple cupcakes
Prepare the basic cupcake recipe. Add 65 g (2½ oz) desiccated coconut to the mixture after it has been creamed.

variations

mini peanut butter cupcakes

see base recipe page 236

mini marshmallow & peanut butter cupcakes
Prepare the basic cupcake recipe. Add 115 g (4 oz) chopped large
marshmallows to the melted chocolate mixture.

mini coconut & peanut butter cupcakes
Prepare the basic cupcake recipe. Add 3 tablespoons desiccated coconut
to the melted chocolate.

mini jam & peanut butter cupcakes
Prepare the basic cupcake recipe. Place a teaspoon of your favourite fruit
jam into the bottom of the baking cases and top with the peanut butter
and then the chocolate.

crisp rice cupcakes

see base recipe page 239

marshmallow & crisp rice cupcakes
Prepare the basic cupcake recipe. Stir in 25 g (1 oz) miniature marshmallows along with the cereal.

raisins & crisp rice cupcakes
Prepare the basic cupcake recipe. Stir in 100 g (3½ oz) raisins along with the cereal.

cherry & crisp rice cupcakes
Prepare the basic cupcake recipe. Stir in 100 g (3½ oz) chopped red glacé cherries along with the cereal.

eggy cupcakes

see base recipe page 240

kiwi cupcakes
Prepare the basic cupcake recipe, substituting 18 thin slices kiwi fruit for the peach halves.

nectarine cupcakes
Prepare the basic cupcake recipe, substituting 18 nectarine halves for the peach halves.

custard (runny egg) cupcakes
Prepare the basic cupcake recipe. Slice a thin circle off the top of each baked and cooled cupcake. Using a teaspoon, make a small hole about 2½ cm (1 in) deep. Pipe 1 teaspoon prepared custard into the hole. Replace the "lid," icing and add the peach half.

chocolate berry cupcakes

see base recipe page 243

chocolate raspberry cupcakes
Prepare the basic cupcake recipe, substituting 100 g (3½ oz) fresh raspberries
for the blackberries.

chocolate blueberry cupcakes
Prepare the basic cupcake recipe, substituting 100 g (3½ oz) fresh blueberries
for the blackberries.

chocolate cherry cupcakes
Prepare the basic cupcake recipe, substituting 100 g (3½ oz) fresh cherries
for the blackberries.

variations

space dust cupcakes

see base recipe page 244

ginger space dust cupcakes
Prepare the basic cupcake recipe, adding 1 teaspoon ground ginger
and 3 tablespoons crystallised ginger to the creamed cupcake batter.

cherry space dust cupcakes
Prepare the basic cupcake recipe, adding 100 g (3½ oz) chopped
glacé cherries to the creamed cupcake batter.

pineapple space dust cupcakes
Prepare the basic cupcake recipe, adding 100 g (3½ oz) chopped
dried pineapple to the creamed cupcake batter.

variations

jelly doughnut cupcakes

see base recipe page 246

boston cream doughnut cupcakes
Prepare the basic cupcake recipe. Substitute 115 ml (4 fl oz) vanilla custard
for the raspberry jam.

chocolate custard doughnut cupcakes
Prepare the basic cupcake recipe. Substitute 115 ml (4 fl oz) chocolate
custard for the raspberry jam.

marmalade doughnut cupcakes
Prepare the basic cupcake recipe. Substitute 150 g (5 oz) orange marmalade
for the raspberry jam.

wholesome muffins

This chapter is packed full of recipes filled with healthy,

good-for-you ingredients. From wholemeal peach muffins

to mini couscous cakes, being healthy never tasted so good!

spinach & pine nut muffins

see variations page 280

This is a wonderful Mediterranean combination and an ideal lunchtime treat.

265 g (9½ oz) plain flour
Pinch of salt
1 tbsp baking powder
2 tbsp caster sugar
¼ tsp nutmeg

240 ml (8½ fl oz) milk
3 tbsp olive oil
1 lightly beaten egg
200 g (7 oz) chopped cooked spinach
100 g (3½ oz) pine nuts

Preheat the oven to 175°C (350°F / Gas mark 4). Grease a large 6-cup muffin tin.

Mix the dry ingredients in a medium bowl. In a large bowl, combine the milk, oil and egg with an electric whisk until well combined. Fold the flour mixture into the milk mixture and stir until nearly combined. Stir in the spinach and pine nuts.

Spoon the batter into the prepared tin. Bake for 20 minutes.

Remove tin from the oven and cool for 5 minutes. Remove the muffins and cool on a rack.

Store in an airtight container for up to 3 days, or freeze for up to 3 months.

Makes ½ dozen muffins

wild rice muffins

see variations page 281

Wild rice is technically a marsh grass, with a fantastic nutty texture.

70 g (2¾ oz) wild rice, soaked in cold water
    for about 2 hours
2 eggs
250 ml (9 fl oz) milk
100 g (3½ oz) unsalted butter, melted
175 g (6 oz) plain flour
70 g (2¾ oz) wheat bran

60 g (2½ oz) brown sugar
1 tbsp baking powder
½ tsp mixed spice
3 tbsp chopped dried prunes
3 tbsp chopped hazelnuts
4 tbsp chopped dried peaches

Drain the wild rice. Place it in a medium saucepan, cover with 450 ml (16 fl oz) cold water, and bring to the boil. Simmer for 50 minutes, until the rice is tender. Drain and rinse under cold water. Set aside to cool.

Preheat the oven to 190°C (375°F / Gas mark 5). Grease a 12-cup muffin tin. In a medium bowl, beat the rice, eggs, milk and butter with an electric whisk until combined. In a large bowl, combine the flour, bran, sugar, baking powder and mixed spice. Add the cooled rice mixture and stir until just combined. Fold in the prunes, hazelnuts and peaches. Spoon the mixture into the prepared tin. Bake for 20 minutes. Remove tin from the oven and cool for 5 minutes. Then remove muffins and cool on a rack.

Store in an airtight container for up to 3 days, or freeze for up to 3 months.

Makes 1 dozen

mini couscous cakes

see variations page 282

Couscous, the world's smallest pasta, is a staple throughout northern Africa. It gives these cakes a light and elegant texture.

90 g (3¼ oz) couscous
115 ml (4 fl oz) boiling water
225 g (8 oz) plain flour
2 tbsp caster sugar
1 tbsp baking powder
Pinch of salt

1 tsp toasted cumin seeds
1 tsp ground coriander
1 egg
4 tbsp olive oil
1 tbsp lemon zest
2 tbsp chopped flat-leaf parsley

Preheat the oven to 175°C (350°F / Gas mark 4). Place 24 mini paper cases in a muffin tin. Put the couscous in a medium bowl and pour the boiling water over it. Cover and leave for 5 minutes, so the grains absorb the liquid. Fluff the grains apart with a fork.

Mix the dry ingredients in a bowl with a spoon. Beat the egg and oil in a large bowl with an electric whisk until combined. Add the couscous and the dry ingredients and mix until nearly combined. Fold in the lemon zest and parsley. Spoon the mixture into the cases. Bake for 20 minutes. Remove tin from the oven and cool for 5 minutes. Then remove the mini cakes and cool on a rack.

Store in an airtight container for up to 3 days, or freeze for up to 3 months.

Makes 2 dozen mini cakes

basil pesto cupcakes

see variations page 283

These unusually savoury cupcakes make an ideal wholesome treat.

for the cupcakes
115 g (4 oz) yellow polenta
115 g (4 oz) plain flour
2 tsp baking powder
3 tbsp sugar
Pinch of salt
2 eggs
225 ml (8 fl oz) whole milk
50 g (2 oz) unsalted butter, melted

for the topping
115 g (4 oz) basil pesto
350 g (12 oz) cream cheese, softened
12 cherry tomatoes

Preheat the oven to 175°C (350°F / Gas mark 4). Place 12 paper baking cases into a muffin tin. In a medium bowl, stir the dry ingredients. Beat the eggs, milk and butter in a large bowl with an electric whisk until combined. Add the flour mixture to the egg mixture, and stir until just combined. Spoon the batter into the cases. Bake for 20 minutes. Remove tin and cool for 5 minutes. Then remove the cupcakes and cool on a rack. For the topping, beat the pesto and cream cheese with an electric whisk until smooth and creamy. Smear the topping onto the cooled cupcakes and garnish with the cherry tomatoes.

Store without topping in an airtight container for up to 3 days, or freeze for up to 3 months.

Makes 1 dozen

vegetable bran muffins

see variations page 284

These muffins are great for children because they contain a host of essential nutrients and vitamins – and yet they taste delicious.

450 g (1 lb) oat bran
115 g (4 oz) self-raising flour
1 tsp baking powder
100 g (3½ oz) brown sugar
Pinch of salt
2 tsp cinnamon

450 ml (16 fl oz) milk
4 tbsp vegetable oil
2 lightly beaten eggs
2 tbsp honey
400 g (14 oz) grated courgettes and carrots
250 g (9 oz) raisins

Preheat the oven to 175°C (350°F / Gas mark 4). Grease a 12-cup muffin tin.

In a large bowl, combine the dry ingredients with a spoon. In a separate bowl, beat the milk, oil, eggs and honey with an electric whisk until combined. Stir in the grated vegetables and raisins. Add the dry ingredients and stir until just combined. Spoon the mixture into the prepared tin.

Bake in the oven for 20 minutes. Remove tin from the oven and cool for 5 minutes. Then remove the muffins and cool on a rack.

Store in an airtight container for up to 3 days, or freeze for up to 3 months.

Makes 1 dozen

wholemeal peach muffins

see variations page 285

Peaches are packed full of vitamins. They have high levels of vitamin A and beta carotene which help keep the immune system strong and combat the signs of ageing.

450 g (1 lb) drained stewed or tinned peaches
100 g (3½ oz) plain flour
90 g (3¼ oz) wholemeal flour
2 tsp baking powder
Pinch of salt

70 g (2¾ oz) brown sugar
1 lightly beaten egg
4 tbsp vegetable oil
115 ml (4 fl oz) whole milk

Preheat the oven to 175°C (350°F / Gas mark 4). Grease a large 6-cup muffin tin.

Purée the peaches in a food processor. In a medium bowl, combine the flours, baking powder, salt and sugar with a spoon. In a large bowl, beat the egg, oil and milk with an electric whisk until combined. Stir in the peach purée, then add the flour mixture and mix until just combined. Spoon the mixture into the prepared tin.

Bake for 20 minutes. Remove tin from the oven and cool for 5 minutes. Then remove the muffins and cool on a rack.

Store in an airtight container for up to 3 days, or freeze for up to 3 months.

Makes ½ dozen

oatmeal muffins

see variations page 286

These hearty muffins make a great start to the day. You won't feel hungry until lunchtime!

225 g (8 oz) plain flour
200 g (7 oz) brown sugar
1 tbsp baking powder
1 tsp cinnamon
40 g (1½ oz) wheat bran
40 g (1½ oz) porridge oats

Pinch of salt
450 ml (16 fl oz) buttermilk
2 lightly beaten eggs
175 ml (6 fl oz) vegetable oil
175 g (6 oz) raisins

Preheat the oven to 175°C (350°F / Gas mark 4). Grease a 12-cup muffin tin.

In a medium bowl, combine the dry ingredients with a spoon. In a large bowl, beat the buttermilk, eggs and oil with an electric whisk until combined.

Add the dry ingredients and stir until almost blended. Fold in the raisins.

Spoon the mixture into the prepared tin. Bake for 20 minutes. Remove tin from the oven and cool for 5 minutes. Then remove the muffins and cool on a rack.

Store in an airtight container for up to 2 days, or freeze for up to 3 months.

Makes 1 dozen

aubergine caviar muffins

see variations page 287

The caviar in the title actually refers to the seeds of the aubergine.

for the cupcakes
2 small aubergines
6 tbsp extra virgin olive oil
375 g (13 oz) plain flour
4 tsp baking powder
Pinch of salt
1 lightly beaten egg
300 ml (10 fl oz) milk

for the butter
115 g (4 oz) unsalted butter, softened
2 cloves finely minced garlic
2 tsp sherry vinegar
Pinch of salt and pepper
1 tbsp chopped parsley

Preheat the oven to 175°C (350°F / Gas mark 4). Rub the aubergines with 2 tablespoons olive oil. Bake on a baking sheet for 30 minutes, until the aubergines soften and turn dark brown. When cool enough to handle, remove the tops and slice lengthwise. Using a spoon, scrape the flesh away from the skin. Discard the skin and roughly chop the aubergine flesh. Set aside.

Grease a 12-cup muffin tin. In a medium bowl, combine the dry ingredients. In a large bowl, beat the egg, milk and remaining olive oil. Mix in the flour until nearly combined. Fold in the chopped aubergine. Spoon the mixture into the prepared tin. Bake for 25 minutes. Remove tin from the oven and cool for 5 minutes. Then remove the muffins and cool on a rack. To make the butter, combine the butter, garlic, vinegar and parsley in a bowl. Beat until well combined, then season with salt and pepper. Serve as an accompaniment to the muffins. Store in an airtight container for up to 2 days, or freeze for up to 3 months.

Makes 1 dozen

pistachio & apricot muffins

see variations page 288

The pistachio is a highly prized nut used throughout the Mediterranean to flavour everything from patés to ice creams.

225 g (8 oz) roughly chopped dried apricots
4 tbsp brandy
450 g (1 lb) self-raising flour
115 g (4 oz) unsalted butter, cubed
115 g (4 oz) caster sugar

2 lightly beaten eggs
175 ml (6 fl oz) buttermilk
50 g (2 oz) chopped pistachios

Soak the chopped apricots in the brandy and let stand for 1 hour.

Preheat the oven to 175°C (350°F / Gas mark 4). Grease a 12-cup muffin tin. Drain the apricots and then purée in a food processor until smooth. Put the flour and butter in a medium bowl. Using your fingertips, rub the butter into the flour until it resembles fine breadcrumbs. Stir in the sugar, eggs, buttermilk and pistachios until just combined.

Spoon the mixture into the prepared tin. Bake for 20 minutes.

Remove tin from the oven and cool for 5 minutes. Remove the muffins and cool on a rack.

Store in an airtight container for up to 3 days, or freeze for up to 3 months.

Makes 1 dozen

pb & banana cupcakes

see variations page 289

This familiar combination makes a truly delicious cupcake.

225 g (8 oz) unsalted butter, softened
200 g (7 oz) caster sugar
115 g (4 oz) self-raising flour
115 g (4 oz) self-raising wholemeal flour
1 tsp baking powder
4 eggs
3 tbsp ground almonds
1 tsp vanilla essence
2 tsp cinnamon

4 tbsp peanut butter chips
250 g (9 oz) mashed bananas

for the icing
200 g (7 oz) cream cheese, softened
175 g (6 oz) icing sugar, sieved
1 tbsp lemon juice
1 tsp of vanilla essence
115 g (4 oz) mashed banana

Preheat the oven to 175°C (350°F / Gas mark 4). Place 24 paper baking cases in muffin tins. Combine the butter, sugar, flours, baking powder, eggs, almonds, vanilla and cinnamon in a large bowl and beat with an electric whisk until smooth and pale, about 2 to 3 minutes. Stir in the peanut butter chips and mashed bananas. Spoon the batter into the paper cases. Bake for 20 minutes. Remove tin and cool for 5 minutes. Remove the cupcakes and cool on a rack.

To make the icing, beat the cream cheese and icing sugar in a medium bowl with an electric whisk until soft and light. Add the lemon juice, vanilla and mashed bananas. Beat until well combined. Spoon the icing over the cupcakes. Store in an airtight container for up to 2 days or freeze for up to 3 months.

Makes 2 dozen

chickpea muffins

see variations page 290

Chickpeas, or garbanzo beans, are full of fibre and make these muffins a great lunchtime treat.

3 tbsp plus 200 g (7 oz) polenta
300 g (10½ oz) self-raising flour
2 tbsp chopped fresh basil
1 tsp baking powder
Pinch of salt

315 ml (10¾ fl oz) milk
1 lightly beaten egg
90 g (3¼ oz) unsalted butter, melted
300 g (10½ oz) drained tinned or cooked
    chickpeas
2 tbsp grated Parmesan cheese

Preheat the oven to 175°C (350°F / Gas mark 4). Grease a 6-cup muffin tin and dust with 3 tablespoons polenta. In a medium bowl, combine the flour, remaining polenta, basil, baking powder and salt with a spoon. In a large bowl, beat the milk, egg and butter with an electric whisk until combined. Add the chickpeas and Parmesan cheese. Add the flour mixture and stir until just combined. Spoon the mixture into the prepared tin. Bake for 25 minutes.

Remove tin and cool for 5 minutes. Then remove the muffins and cool on a rack.

Store in an airtight container for up to 3 days, or freeze for up to 3 months.

Makes ¹/₂ dozen

date & pecan muffins

see variations page 291

With over 40 different named varieties, the date fruit of the palm tree comes in many different textures and flavours. For this muffin try using Medjool dates, which have a thick flesh and a dark, rich flavour.

275 g (10 oz) plain flour
115 g (4 oz) caster sugar
1 tbsp baking powder
2 eggs
4 tbsp butter, melted

60 ml (2½ fl oz) soured cream
2 tbsp milk
1 large mashed banana
150 g (5 oz) chopped dates
4 tbsp chopped pecans

Preheat the oven to 175°C (350°F / Gas mark 4). Grease a 12-cup muffin tin.

In a medium bowl, combine the flour, sugar and baking powder with a spoon.

In a large bowl, beat the eggs, butter, soured cream, milk and banana with an electric whisk until combined. Fold in the flour mixture until just combined. Stir in the dates and pecan nuts.

Spoon the mixture into the prepared tin. Bake for 20 minutes. Remove tin from the oven and cool for 5 minutes. Then remove the muffins and cool on a rack.

Store in an airtight container for up to 3 days, or freeze for up to 3 months.

Makes 1 dozen

variations

spinach & pine nut muffins

see base recipe page 261

pesto & pine nut muffins
Prepare the basic muffin recipe, substituting 60 g (2½ oz) fresh basil pesto for the spinach.

spinach, pine nut & black olive muffins
Prepare the basic muffin recipe, adding 60 g (2½ oz) finely chopped black olives along with the spinach and pine nuts.

spinach & parmesan muffins
Prepare the basic muffin recipe, mixing 4 tablespoons freshly grated Parmesan cheese in with the spinach and pine nuts. Sprinkle ½ teaspoon Parmesan on top of each muffin before baking.

variations

wild rice muffins

see base recipe page 262

wild rice & date muffins
Prepare the basic muffin recipe, substituting 3 tablespoons chopped dates for the chopped prunes.

wild rice & apricot muffins
Prepare the basic muffin recipe, substituting 4 tablespoons chopped dried apricots for the chopped peaches.

wild rice & berry muffins
Prepare the basic muffin recipe, substituting 1½ tablespoons dried blueberries, 1½ tablespoons dried cranberries and 1½ tablespoons dried cherries for the chopped peaches.

variations

mini couscous cakes

see base recipe page 265

mini couscous & coriander cakes
Prepare the basic cupcake recipe, adding 2 tablespoons freshly chopped coriander along with the lemon zest and parsley.

mini couscous cakes with preserved lemon & thyme
Prepare the basic cupcake recipe, adding 1 teaspoon chopped preserved lemon and 1 tablespoon chopped thyme leaves along with the lemon zest and parsley.

mini couscous cakes with olive & chilli
Prepare the basic cupcake recipe, adding 3 tablespoons tapenade or olive paste and 1 teaspoon chopped chilli pepper along with the lemon zest and parsley.

basil pesto cupcakes

see base recipe page 266

basil pesto & coriander cupcakes
Prepare the basic cupcake recipe, adding 3 tablespoons finely chopped coriander to the topping.

red pepper pesto cupcakes
Prepare the basic cupcake recipe, substituting 115 g (4 oz) red pepper pesto for the basil pesto.

basil pesto & chilli cupcakes
Prepare the basic cupcake recipe, adding 1 teaspoon chilli flakes to the batter before it has been mixed together.

variations

vegetable bran muffins

see base recipe page 268

feta & vegetable bran muffins
Prepare the basic muffin recipe, folding in 75 g (3 oz) crumbled feta cheese after adding the vegetables and raisins.

apple bran muffins
Prepare the basic muffin recipe, substituting 200 g (7 oz) grated apple for the grated courgettes.

thyme bran muffins
Prepare the basic muffin recipe, adding 1 tablespoon fresh thyme along with the vegetables and raisins.

variations

wholemeal peach muffins

see base recipe page 269

wholemeal apricot muffins
Prepare the basic muffin recipe, substituting 400 g (14 oz) fresh or tinned apricot for the peaches.

wholemeal pear muffins
Prepare the basic muffin recipe, substituting 400 g (14 oz) fresh or tinned pears for the peaches.

wholemeal nectarine muffins
Prepare the basic muffin recipe, substituting 400 g (14 oz) fresh or tinned nectarines for the peaches.

variations

oatmeal muffins

see base recipe page 270

raspberry oatmeal muffins
Prepare the basic muffin recipe, substituting 200 g (7 oz) dried raspberries for the raisins.

blueberry oatmeal muffins
Prepare the basic muffin recipe, substituting 200 g (7 oz) dried blueberries for the raisins.

cranberry oatmeal muffins
Prepare the basic muffin recipe, substituting 200 g (7 oz) dried cranberries for the raisins.

variations

aubergine caviar muffins

see base recipe page 273

red pepper & aubergine muffins
Prepare the basic muffin recipe, adding 3 tablespoons minced red pepper along with adding the aubergine.

raisin & cinnamon aubergine muffins
Prepare the basic muffin recipe, adding 100 g (3½ oz) raisins and 2 teaspoons cinnamon along with the aubergine.

sesame seed & aubergine muffins
Prepare the basic muffin recipe, adding 3 tablespoons tahini paste before folding in the aubergine.

variations

pistachio & apricot muffins

see base recipe page 274

pecan & apricot muffins
Prepare the basic muffin recipe, substituting 3 tablespoons chopped pecans for the pistachios.

pistachio & peach muffins
Prepare the basic muffin recipe, substituting 225 g (8 oz) dried peaches for the apricots.

walnut & apricot muffins
Prepare the basic muffin recipe, substituting 3 tablespoons chopped walnuts for the pistachios.

pb & banana cupcakes

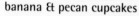

see base recipe page 276

banana & pecan cupcakes
Prepare the basic cupcake recipe, substituting 4 tablespoons of chopped pecans for the peanut butter chips.

pb & banana cupcakes with maple syrup & ginger icing
Prepare the basic cupcake recipe. In the icing, substitute 4 tablespoons maple syrup for the icing sugar. Stir in 3 tablespoons chopped crystallised ginger along with the peanut butter chips and mashed banana.

banana, peanut butter & chocolate chip cupcakes
Prepare the basic cupcake recipe, adding 4 tablespoons of plain chocolate chips after creaming the batter.

variations

chickpea muffins

see base recipe page 277

mixed herb muffins
Prepare the basic muffin recipe, adding 1 tablespoon each chopped fresh flat leaf parsley, fresh chives and fresh thyme to the dry ingredients.

chilli muffins
Prepare the basic muffin recipe, adding 1 teaspoon fresh chilli flakes to the dry ingredients.

roasted garlic butter muffins
Prepare the basic muffin recipe. Serve with roasted garlic butter. Mix 2 tablespoons minced roasted garlic with 125 g (4½ oz) unsalted butter, 1 tablespoon chopped parsley and 1 teaspoon lemon zest.

variations

date & pecan muffins

see base recipe page 278

date & pecan muffins with maple syrup butter
Prepare the basic muffin recipe and serve with orange and maple syrup butter. Mix 1 teaspoon orange essence with 2 tablespoons maple syrup. Combine with 225 g (4½ oz) softened, unsalted butter.

date & pistachio muffins
Prepare the basic muffin recipe, substituting 4 tablespoons chopped pistachios for the pecans.

date & macadamia nut muffins
Prepare the basic muffin recipe, substituting 4 tablespoons chopped macadamia nuts for the pecans.

low-fat cupcakes

Moist and sweet banana and honey cupcakes, spicy and earthy

pumpkin and ginger muffins – you'll never know these flavourful

cupcakes are low in fat!

ricotta cheesecake cupcakes

see variations page 314

Ricotta cheese is lower in fat than cream cheese and it has a great texture.

125 g (4½ oz) digestive biscuit crumbs
3 tbsp margarine, melted
2 tbsp honey
900 g (2 lb) semi-skimmed ricotta cheese

4 eggs
175 g (6 oz) icing sugar, sieved
1 tsp orange essence
75 g (3 oz) walnut halves

Preheat the oven to 160°C (325°F / Gas mark 3). Place 12 paper baking cases in a muffin tin.

In a food processor, combine the biscuit crumbs, margarine and honey. Spoon 1 tablespoon of the mixture into each case, pressing firmly into the bottom. Chill until set.

In a large bowl, beat the ricotta with an electric whisk until soft. Then beat in the eggs, icing sugar and orange essence. Fold in the walnuts. Spoon the mixture into the cases.

Bake in the oven for 25 minutes. Remove tin from the oven and cool for 5 minutes. Then remove the cupcakes and cool on a rack. Chill until ready to serve.

Store covered in the refrigerator for up to 2 days.

Makes 1 dozen

raspberry & cottage cheese muffins

see variations page 315

These muffins make a delicious treat whether you are counting fat grammes or not!

300 g (10½ oz) plain flour
175 g (6 oz) caster sugar
1 tbsp baking powder
Pinch of salt
2 lightly beaten eggs

4 tbsp sunflower oil
250 ml (9 fl oz) low-fat milk
115 g (4 oz) low-fat cottage cheese
150 g (5 oz) fresh raspberries

Preheat the oven to 175°C (350°F / Gas mark 4). Grease a 12-cup muffin tin.

In a medium bowl, mix the flour, sugar, baking powder and salt with a spoon.

In a large bowl, beat the eggs, oil, milk and cottage cheese with an electric whisk until smooth. Add the flour mixture and stir until nearly combined. Fold in the raspberries, but do not overmix. Spoon the mixture into the prepared tin. Bake in the oven for 20 minutes.

Remove tin from the oven and cool for 5 minutes. Remove the muffins and cool on a rack.

Store in an airtight container for up to 2 days, or freeze for up to 3 months.

Makes 1 dozen

low-fat chocolate chip muffins

see variations page 316

These low-fat chocolate treats won't tip the balance on the scales.

for the muffins
300 g (10½ oz) plain flour
225 g (8 oz) caster sugar
1 tbsp baking powder
2 tbsp Dutch-process cocoa powder
2 lightly beaten eggs
115 ml (4 fl oz) sunflower oil
175 ml (6 fl oz) fat-free milk
1 tsp vanilla essence

for the icing
2 tbsp margarine, softened
175 g (6 oz) icing sugar, sieved
30 g (1¼ oz) Dutch-process cocoa powder
½ tsp orange essence
½ tsp vanilla essence
4 tbsp fat-free milk

Preheat the oven to 175°C (350°F / Gas mark 4). Grease a 12-cup muffin tin. In a medium bowl, mix the flour, sugar, baking powder and cocoa with a spoon. In a large bowl, combine the eggs, oil, milk and vanilla with an electric whisk and beat until combined. Add the flour mixture and stir until just combined. Do not overmix. Spoon the batter into the prepared tin. Bake for 20 minutes. Remove tin from the oven and cool for 5 minutes. Then remove the muffins and cool on a rack. For the icing, combine all the ingredients except the milk. Add the milk slowly, beating with an electric whisk to make a firm but spreadable mixture. Spoon the icing onto the cooled muffins.

Store without icing in an airtight container for up to 3 days, or freeze for up to 3 months.

Makes 1 dozen

low-fat vanilla cupcakes

see variations page 317

After you have used the seeds from the vanilla bean, put the pod into an airtight jar and pour caster sugar on top. In a few weeks you will have vanilla sugar!

for the cupcakes
3 egg yolks
225 g (8 oz) caster sugar
1 vanilla bean, pod removed
50 ml (2 fl oz) cold water
115 g (4 oz) cake flour
1 tsp baking powder
Pinch of salt

5 egg whites
⅛ tsp cream of tartar

for the glaze
175 g (6 oz) icing sugar
1 tsp vanilla essence
2 tbsp lemon juice
1 tbsp poppy seeds

Preheat the oven to 175°C (350°F / Gas mark 4). Place 12 paper baking cases in a muffin tin. In a large bowl, beat the egg yolks and half the sugar until pale and creamy. Then add the vanilla seeds. Add the water, flour, baking powder and salt to the egg mixture and beat with an electric mixer until just combined. In a medium bowl, combine the egg whites and cream of tartar. Beat with an electric whisk until soft peaks form. Add the remaining sugar, one-third at a time, beating well after each addition. Using a metal spoon, gently fold the egg whites into the batter. Spoon the mixture into the cases and bake for 20 minutes. To make the glaze, sieve the icing sugar in a bowl. Add the vanilla essence, lemon juice and poppy seeds and beat until creamy and slightly runny. Drizzle the glaze over the cupcakes. Store in an airtight container for up to 2 days, or freeze for up to 3 months.

Makes 1 dozen

flour-lite chocolate cupcakes

see variations page 318

This recipe has only a small amount of flour to give the cupcakes a light, fluffy texture.

50 g (2 oz) Dutch-process cocoa powder
150 g (5 oz) light brown sugar
3 tbsp plain flour
Pinch of salt
1 tsp vanilla essence
1 tsp orange essence
175 ml (6 fl oz) fat-free milk

115 g (4 oz) chopped plain dark chocolate
1 lightly beaten egg
3 egg whites
¼ tsp cream of tartar
75 g (3 oz) caster sugar
Cocoa powder, for dusting
Icing sugar, for dusting

In a heavy-based saucepan, combine the cocoa, sugar, flour, salt, vanilla, orange essence and milk over a gentle heat. Stir until the sugar dissolves, being careful not to burn the mixture. Remove from the heat, and gradually stir in the chocolate until it melts. Whisk in the egg. Transfer to a large bowl to cool, and set aside. Preheat the oven to 175°C (350°F / Gas mark 4). Place 12 paper baking cases in a muffin tin. In a medium bowl, combine the egg whites and cream of tartar. Beat with an electric whisk until soft peaks form. Gradually add the sugar, one-third at a time, beating for 1 minute after each addition. Using a metal spoon, fold the egg whites into the chocolate, making sure not to overmix. Spoon the mixture into the cases. Bake for 20 minutes. Remove the tin from the oven and cool for 5 minutes. Then remove the cupcakes, dust with cocoa and icing sugar, and serve immediately.

Store in an airtight container for up to 2 days, or freeze for up to 3 months.

Makes 1 dozen

quick apple sauce cupcakes

see variations page 319

Simple to make and low in fat, this recipe is based on the classic streusel cake.

for the cupcakes
115 g (4 oz) margarine, softened
150 g (5 oz) light brown sugar
1 lightly beaten egg
175 g (6 oz) unsweetened apple sauce
225 g (8 oz) self-raising flour
1 tsp baking powder
1 tsp ground ginger
¼ tsp ground cloves

for the topping
2 tbsp margarine, softened
30 g (1¼ oz) icing sugar, sieved
3 tbsp chopped walnuts
2 tbsp porridge oats
2 tbsp plain flour
½ tsp cinnamon

Preheat the oven to 175°C (350°F / Gas mark 4). Place 12 paper baking cases in a muffin tin. In a medium bowl, beat the margarine and sugar with an electric whisk until pale and creamy. Slowly add the egg and then the apple sauce, beating well after each addition. Add the flour, baking powder and spices, mixing until just combined. To make the topping, combine all the ingredients in a small bowl. Mix with a fork until the topping resembles coarse breadcrumbs. Set aside. Spoon the batter into the cases. Sprinkle some topping on each cupcake and bake for 20 to 25 minutes. Remove tin from the oven and cool for 5 minutes. Then remove the cupcakes and cool on a rack.

Store in an airtight container for up to 3 days, or freeze for up to 3 months.

Makes 1 dozen

glazed blueberry-lime cupcakes

see variations page 320

Low in fat with super-food blueberries – you may feel virtuous when you bake these!

for the cupcakes
115 g (4 oz) margarine, softened
225 g (8 oz) caster sugar
2 lightly beaten eggs
1 tsp vanilla essence
115 ml (4 fl oz) fat-free milk
225 g (8 oz) self-raising flour
1 tsp baking powder

115 g (4 oz) fresh blueberries
1 tbsp grated lime zest

for the glaze
115 g (4 oz) caster sugar
2 tbsp grated lime zest
3 tbsp lime juice
2 tbsp boiling water

Preheat the oven to 175°C (350°F / Gas mark 4). Place 18 paper baking cases in muffin tins. Combine the margarine and sugar with an electric whisk until soft and creamy. Add the eggs slowly and mix well. Beat in the vanilla and milk. Sieve the flour and baking powder and stir into the batter until just combined. Fold in the blueberries and lime zest. Spoon the mixture into the cases. Bake for 20 minutes. Remove tins from the oven and cool for 5 minutes. Then remove the cupcakes and cool on a rack. To make the glaze, mix the sugar, lime zest, lime juice and boiling water in a small saucepan. Bring to a gentle simmer over a medium heat, stirring to dissolve the sugar. Simmer uncovered for 5 minutes. Remove from the heat, cool slightly and spoon over the cool cupcakes. Store in an airtight container for up to 3 days, or unglazed in the freezer for up to 3 months.

Makes 1½ dozen

banana & honey cupcakes

see variations page 321

Bananas lend themselves to natural sweeteners like maple syrup and honey. Add walnuts to offset the sweetness and to give the cupcakes a little crunch.

450 g (1 lb) mashed bananas
150 g (5 oz) light brown sugar
90 g (3¼ oz) honey
4 tbsp margarine, melted

225 g (8 oz) self-raising flour
1 tsp baking powder
Pinch of salt
150 g (5 oz) roughly chopped walnuts

Preheat the oven to 175°C (350°F / Gas mark 4). Place 18 paper baking cases in muffin tins.

In a large bowl, combine the bananas, sugar, honey and margarine. Beat with an electric whisk until well blended. Slowly add the flour, baking powder and salt and mix well. Fold in the chopped walnuts.

Spoon the batter into the cases. Bake for 20 minutes. Remove tins from the oven and cool for 5 minutes. Remove the cupcakes and cool on a rack.

Store in an airtight container for up to 2 days, or freeze for up to 3 months.

Makes 1½ dozen

pumpkin & ginger muffins

see variations page 322

These muffins are a delicious autumnal treat. If you can't find fresh pumpkin, then try using tinned pumpkin.

300 g (10½ oz) plain flour
75 g (3 oz) light brown sugar
1 tbsp baking powder
½ tsp nutmeg
½ tsp ground cloves
1 tsp ground ginger
Pinch of salt

1 lightly beaten egg
115 g (4 oz) puréed pumpkin, fresh or tinned
75 ml (3 fl oz) fat-free milk
40 ml (1½ fl oz) sunflower oil
3 tbsp chopped crystallised ginger
4 tbsp pumpkin seeds

Preheat the oven to 175°C (350°F / Gas mark 4). Grease a 12-cup muffin tin. In a medium bowl, combine the dry ingredients with a spoon.

In a large bowl, beat the egg, pumpkin, milk, and oil with an electric whisk until well combined. Add the flour mixture to the pumpkin mixture, mixing until nearly combined. Fold in the crystallised ginger, but do not overmix. Spoon the batter into the prepared tin.

Sprinkle each muffin with a few of the pumpkin seeds. Bake for 20 minutes. Remove tin from the oven and cool for 5 minutes. Then remove the muffins and cool on a rack.

Store in an airtight container for up to 2 days, or freeze for up to 3 months.

Makes 1 dozen

marbled mini bundt cakes

see variations page 323

Bake these cakes in little bundt tins for a really extravagant-looking cupcake. You can also use ordinary muffin tins.

115 g (4 oz) margarine, softened
225 g (8 oz) caster sugar
2 lightly beaten eggs
1 tsp vanilla essence
175 g (6 oz) plain flour

1 tbsp baking powder
175 ml (6 fl oz) fat-free milk
2 tbsp Dutch-process cocoa powder
100 g (3½ oz) finely chopped plain chocolate
Cocoa powder for dusting

Preheat the oven to 175°C (350°F / Gas mark 4). Grease 6 mini bundt tins or a large 6-cup muffin tins. In a large bowl, beat the margarine and sugar with an electric whisk until thick and pale. Slowly add the eggs and vanilla, beating well. Mix the flour and baking powder in a medium bowl. Add to the margarine mixture in thirds, alternating with the milk.

Divide the batter into two bowls. Fold the cocoa and chocolate into one of the bowls. Spoon a little plain batter into the bottom of the each bundt tin, then spoon some chocolate batter on top. Continue until each tin is three-quarters full and there are 4 layers. Swirl the mixture in each tin using the point of a knife. Bake for 35 minutes. Remove tins from the oven and cool for 10 minutes. Then remove the bundt cakes and cool on a rack. Serve dusted with cocoa. Store in an airtight container for up to 2 days.

Makes ½ dozen

low-fat carrot & nut cupcakes

see variations page 324

The low-fat version of a classic American cake. If you can't get fat-free cream cheese for the icing, use fat-free plain yoghurt.

for the cupcakes
225 g (8 oz) self-raising flour
1 tsp baking powder
¹/₂ tsp nutmeg
1 tsp ground ginger
150 g (5 oz) brown sugar
100 g (3¹/₂ oz) grated carrots
100 g (3¹/₂ oz) roughly chopped walnuts
200 g (7 oz) mashed bananas

2 lightly beaten eggs
175 ml (6 fl oz) vegetable oil

for the icing
200 g (7 oz) fat-free cream cheese, softened
115 g (4 oz) icing sugar, sieved
1 tsp vanilla essence
4 tbsp chopped walnuts
12 walnut halves

Preheat the oven to 175°C (350°F / Gas mark 4). Place 12 paper baking cases in a muffin tin. In a large bowl, combine all the cupcake ingredients. Beat on a low speed with an electric whisk until all the ingredients are combined. Spoon the mixture into the cases until two-thirds full. Bake for 20 minutes. Remove tin from the oven and cool for 5 minutes. Remove the cupcakes and cool on a rack. To make the icing, combine the cream cheese with the icing sugar and vanilla with an electric whisk. Beat until smooth and creamy. Fold in the walnuts. Smear onto the cooled cupcakes and garnish with the walnut halves. Store without icing in an airtight container for up to 3 days, or freeze for up to 3 months.

Makes 1 dozen

citrus yoghurt muffins

see variations page 325

The acidity of the yoghurt, balanced with the subtle sweetness of the citrus oils, makes these muffins utterly mouth-watering.

200 g (8 oz) plain flour
175 g (6 oz) caster sugar
1 tbsp grated lemon zest
1 tbsp grated orange zest
1 tbsp grated lime zest

1 tbsp baking powder
Pinch of salt
225 ml (8 fl oz) fat-free plain yoghurt
115 ml (4 fl oz) sunflower oil
1 lightly beaten egg

Preheat the oven to 200°C (400°F / Gas mark 6). Grease a 12-cup muffin tin.

In a medium bowl, combine the flour, sugar, lemon zest, orange zest, lime zest, baking powder and salt. In a large bowl, beat the yoghurt, oil and egg until well blended. Add the flour mixture, stirring until just combined. Do not overmix.

Spoon the batter into the prepared pan. Bake for 20 minutes. Remove tin from the oven and cool for 5 minutes. Then remove the muffins and serve warm.

Store in an airtight container for up to 3 days, or freeze for up to 3 months.

Makes 1 dozen

variations

ricotta cheesecake cupcakes

see base recipe page 293

banana & raisin ricotta cupcakes
Prepare the basic recipe but use only 750 g (1 lb 10 oz) ricotta cheese.
Add 225 g (8 oz) mashed bananas to the ricotta cheese after adding the
eggs and icing sugar. Add 75 g (3 oz) raisins along with the walnuts.

blueberry ricotta cupcakes
Prepare the basic cheesecake mixture, folding in 150 g (5 oz) fresh
blueberries just before adding the walnuts.

raspberry & lime ricotta cupcakes
Prepare the basic cheesecake mixture, folding in 150 g (5 oz) fresh
raspberries and 1 tablespoon freshly grated lime zest just before adding
the walnuts.

variations

raspberry & cottage cheese muffins

see base recipe page 295

blueberry & cottage cheese muffins
Prepare the basic muffin recipe, substituting 150 g (5 oz) fresh blueberries
for the raspberries.

cherry & cottage cheese muffins
Prepare the basic muffin recipe, substituting 150 g (5 oz) fresh cherries
for the raspberries.

apricot & cottage cheese muffins
Prepare the basic muffin recipe, substituting 150 g (5 oz) sliced fresh
apricots for the raspberries.

variations

low-fat chocolate chip muffins

see base recipe page 296

low-fat hazelnut-chocolate muffins
Prepare the basic muffin recipe, adding 3 tablespoons chopped roasted hazelnuts after adding the dry ingredients.

low-fat raspberry-chocolate muffins
Prepare the basic muffin recipe, adding 75 g (3 oz) fresh raspberries to the batter after adding the dry ingredients.

low-fat courgette & chocolate muffins
Prepare the basic muffin recipe. Add 1 teaspoon freshly ground black pepper to the dry ingredients. Add 75 g (3 oz) grated fresh courgettes after mixing in the dry ingredients.

variations

low-fat vanilla cupcakes

see base recipe page 298

low-fat cupcakes with fennel & orange drizzle
Prepare the basic cupcake mixture. In the glaze, substitute 2 teaspoons
lightly crushed fennel seeds for the poppy seeds, and substitute
1 teaspoon orange essence for the vanilla essence.

low-fat cupcakes with strawberry & lime drizzle
Prepare the basic cupcake mixture. In the glaze, substitute 1 teaspoon
strawberry essence for the vanilla, and add 1 tablespoon freshly grated
lime zest to the mixture.

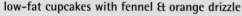

low-fat cupcakes with almond & cherry drizzle
Prepare the basic cupcake mixture. In the glaze, substitute 1 teaspoon
almond essence for the vanilla essence. Add 2 tablespoons chopped
glacé cherries.

variations

flour-lite chocolate cupcakes

see base recipe page 299

flour-lite orange cupcakes
Prepare the basic cupcake recipe, substituting 2 teaspoons orange essence
for the vanilla essence.

flour-lite chocolate-glazed cupcakes
Prepare the basic cupcake recipe. Make a glaze: sift 175 g (6 oz) icing
sugar and 2 tablespoons Dutch-process cocoa powder into a medium bowl.
Beat 2 tablespoons softened margarine into the cocoa powder mixture,
adding 1 tablespoon warm water and 1 tablespoon coffee liqueur to make
a pourable consistency. Spoon over the cupcakes.

flour-lite chocolate & cinnamon cupcakes
Prepare the basic cupcake recipe, adding 2 teaspoons cinnamon to
the dry ingredients.

variations

quick apple sauce cupcakes

see base recipe page 301

pecan & apple sauce cupcakes
Prepare the basic cupcake recipe, adding 3 tablespoons chopped pecans
after adding the dry ingredients. For the topping, substitute 3 tablespoons
chopped pecans for the walnuts.

raisin & apple sauce cupcakes
Prepare the basic cupcake recipe, adding 4 tablespoons raisins after adding
the dry ingredients.

cranberry & apple sauce cupcakes
Prepare the basic cupcake recipe, adding 4 tablespoons dried cranberries
after adding the dry ingredients.

variations

glazed blueberry–lime cupcakes

see base recipe page 302

glazed raspberry-lemon cupcakes
Prepare the basic cupcake recipe, substituting 150 g (5 oz) fresh raspberries for the blueberries, and 1 tablespoon grated lemon zest for the lime zest in the glaze.

glazed blackberry-orange cupcakes
Prepare the basic cupcake recipe, substituting 150 g (5 oz) fresh blackberries for the blueberries, and 1 tablespoon grated orange zest for the lime zest in the glaze.

glazed strawberry-lime cupcakes
Prepare the basic cupcake recipe, substituting 150 g (5 oz) fresh sliced strawberries for the blueberries.

banana & honey cupcakes

see base recipe page 305

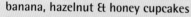

banana, hazelnut & honey cupcakes
Prepare the basic cupcake recipe, substituting 115 g (4 oz) roughly chopped unblanched hazelnuts for the walnuts.

banana & maple syrup cupcakes
Prepare the basic cupcake recipe, substituting 90 g (3¼ oz) maple syrup for the honey.

banana, pecan & golden syrup cupcakes
Prepare the basic cupcake recipe, substituting 115 g (4 oz) roughly chopped pecans for the walnuts, and 90 g (3¼ oz) golden syrup for the honey.

variations

pumpkin & ginger muffins

see base recipe page 306

marjoram, pumpkin & feta cheese muffins
Prepare the basic muffin recipe, substituting 2 teaspoons chopped fresh marjoram for the nutmeg, ginger and cloves. Add 115 g (4 oz) crumbled feta to the batter after the flour has been added.

currant, pumpkin & ginger muffins
Prepare the basic muffin recipe, folding in 100 g (3½ oz) currants along with the crystallised ginger.

pumpkin, ginger, chilli & coriander muffins
Prepare the basic muffin recipe, adding 1 tablespoon freshly minced chilli and 1 tablespoon roughly chopped fresh coriander.

variations

marbled mini bundt cakes

see base recipe page 309

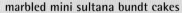

marbled mini sultana bundt cakes
Prepare the basic cupcake recipe. After dividing the batters add
3 tablespoons sultanas to the plain batter.

marbled mini orange & walnut bundt cakes
Prepare the basic cupcake recipe. After dividing the batters add
1 teaspoon orange essence to the chocolate batter, and 3 tablespoons
chopped walnuts to the plain batter.

marbled mini pistachio bundt cakes
Prepare the basic cupcake recipe. After dividing the batters, add
3 tablespoons chopped pistachio nuts to the plain batter.

variations

low-fat carrot & nut cupcakes

see base recipe page 310

low-fat carrot & pecan cupcakes
Prepare the basic cupcake mixture, substituting 75 g (3 oz) of roughly chopped pecans for the walnuts. Substitute 4 tablespoons chopped pecans for the walnuts in the icing, and substitute 12 pecans for the walnut halves for garnishing.

low-fat ginger-iced carrot cupcakes
Prepare the basic cupcake mixture. In the icing, substitute 3 tablespoons chopped crystallised ginger for the chopped walnuts.

low-fat carrot & orange cupcakes
Prepare the basic cupcake mixture, adding 1 teaspoon orange essence and 1 teaspoon ground cumin to the cupcakes.

variations

citrus yoghurt muffins

see base recipe page 313

poppy-seed yoghurt muffins
Prepare the basic muffin recipe, folding in 3 tablespoons of poppy seeds
after adding the dry ingredients.

citrus-glazed yoghurt muffins
Prepare the basic muffin recipe. To make the citrus glaze, combine
1 tablespoon each of lime, orange and lemon zest with 5 tablespoons
water and 115 g (4 oz) caster sugar. Dissolve the sugar in a pan over low
heat. Simmer for 5 minutes. Spoon over the muffins.

citrus & blueberry yoghurt muffins
Prepare the basic muffin recipe, folding in 90 g (3¼ oz) dried blueberries
after adding the dry ingredients.

cupcakes for special diets

Dairy-free berry cupcakes, gluten-free pecan cupcakes,

sugar-free muffins, and chocolate vegan cupcakes –

anyone with special dietary requirements will be well

catered for with the selection of recipes in this chapter.

ultimate flourless choc cupcakes

see variations page 346

For maximum luxury, top with chocolate whipped cream.

for the cupcakes
300 g (10½ oz) plain chocolate chips
225 g (8 oz) unsalted butter
4 eggs
4 egg yolks
115 g (4 oz) caster sugar
2 tbsp Dutch-process cocoa powder, sieved
2 tbsp ground almonds
1 tsp vanilla essence

for the icing
2 tbsp Dutch-process cocoa powder
4 tbsp icing sugar
350 ml (12 fl oz) whipping cream
1 tsp vanilla essence
½ tsp orange essence

Preheat the oven to 190°C (375°F / Gas mark 5). Place 12 paper baking cases in a muffin tin. Put the chocolate and butter in a medium bowl over a pan of simmering water, and stir until melted. Set aside to cool. In a large bowl, cream the eggs and sugar with an electric whisk until pale and thick. Gently fold in the melted chocolate and remaining ingredients. Spoon the batter into the cases. Bake for 20 minutes. Remove tin from the oven and cool for 5 minutes. Remove the cupcakes and cool on a rack. To make the icing, sieve the cocoa and icing sugar together into a medium bowl. Add the cream, vanilla and orange essence. Beat until soft, but the cream should still hold its shape. Spoon over the warm cupcakes.

Store without icing in an airtight container for up to 2 days.

Makes 1 dozen

chocolate vegan cupcakes

see variations page 347

To make this authentically vegan you must use specially labelled vegan chocolate chips.

275 g (10 oz) plain flour
4 tbsp Dutch-process cocoa powder
Pinch of salt
450 g (1 lb) caster sugar
90 g (3¼ oz) unsweetened apple sauce

450 ml (16 fl oz) cold water
2 tsp white vinegar
2 tsp bicarbonate of soda
175 g (6 oz) vegan plain chocolate chips
Cocoa powder, for dusting

Preheat the oven to 190°C (375°F / Gas mark 5). Place 12 paper baking cases in a muffin tin. Sieve the flour, cocoa, salt and sugar into a large bowl and set aside.

In a separate large bowl, combine the apple sauce, water, vinegar and bicarbonate of soda. Add the flour mixture and stir well to combine. Fold in the chocolate chips.

Spoon the mixture into the cases. Bake for about 20 minutes. Remove tin from the oven and cool for 5 minutes. Then remove the cupcakes and cool on a rack.

Serve dusted with cocoa powder.

Store in an airtight container for up to 3 days, or freeze for up to 3 months.

Makes 1 dozen

g.i. carrot cupcakes

see variations page 348

The cupcakes are perfect for those using the glycaemic index to monitor their diet. Low glycaemic foods release their sugars slowly – and are thus more beneficial for maintaining blood sugar levels.

115 ml (4 fl oz) light vegetable oil
115 g (4 oz) brown sugar
1 lightly beaten egg
3 egg whites
190 g (6½ oz) grated carrots
190 g (6½ oz) grated cooking apples
225 g (8 oz) raisins

115 g (4 oz) chopped dates
115 g (4 oz) mixed dried berries
115 g (4 oz) chopped walnuts
1 tsp mixed spice
1 tsp baking powder
350 g (12 oz) self-raising wholemeal flour

Preheat the oven to 175°C (350°F / Gas mark 4). Place 12 paper baking cases into a muffin tin. In a large bowl, combine the oil and sugar, and beat with an electric whisk until light and smooth, about 2 to 3 minutes. Beat the egg and egg whites, one at a time, and then add the carrots, apples, dried fruits and walnuts. Sieve the rest of the ingredients into a medium mixing bowl. Add them to the carrot mixture, stirring until just combined. Spoon the mixture into the cases. Bake for 20 minutes. Remove tin from the oven and cool for 5 minutes. Then remove the cupcakes and cool on a rack. Serve with a low-fat margarine spread.

Store in an airtight container for up to 3 days, or freeze for up to 3 months.

Makes 1 dozen

egg-free chocolate cupcakes

see variations page 349

These deliciously moist, egg-free cupcakes are simple to prepare. The cherry cola lends a subtle sweetness.

225 g (8 oz) unsalted butter, softened
400 g (14 oz) tin condensed milk
225 g (8 oz) self-raising flour
115 g (4 oz) Dutch-process cocoa powder

2 tsp baking powder
100 g (3½ oz) plain chocolate chips
1 tsp vanilla essence
340 ml (11½ fl oz) cherry cola

Preheat the oven to 175°C (350°F / Gas mark 4). Place 12 paper baking cases into a muffin tin.

In a medium bowl, cream the butter with an electric whisk until light, about 2 to 3 minutes. Add the condensed milk and beat until combined. Sieve the flour, cocoa and baking powder into the wet mixture. Stir in the chocolate chips, vanilla and cola.

Spoon the batter into the cases.

Bake for 20 minutes. Remove tin from the oven and cool for 5 minutes. Then remove the cupcakes and cool on a rack.

Store in an airtight container for up to 3 days, or freeze for up to 3 months.

Makes 1 dozen

soy milk muffins

see variations page 350

Soy milk is a perfect replacement for cow's milk. It is fortified with all the vitamins and minerals of its dairy counterpart.

150 g (5 oz) wholemeal flour
1 tbsp baking powder
175 g (6 oz) raisins
1 tsp chopped fresh rosemary
60 g (2½ oz) chopped blanched almonds

60 g (2½ oz) chopped pecans
1 tsp orange essence
115 ml (4 fl oz) olive oil
115 ml (4 fl oz) soy milk
175 g (6 oz) honey

Preheat the oven to 200°C (400°F / Gas mark 6). Grease a 12-cup muffin tin.

In a medium bowl, mix the flour, baking powder, raisins, rosemary, almonds and pecans. In a large bowl, beat the orange essence, oil, soy milk and honey until combined. Slowly fold the dry ingredients into the soy mixture until just combined. Spoon the mixture into the prepared tin.

Bake for 20 minutes. Remove tin from the oven and cool for 5 minutes. Then remove the muffins and cool on a rack.

Store in an airtight container for up to 2 days, or freeze for up to 3 months.

Makes 1 dozen

sugar-free grain muffins

see variations page 351

These great little muffins are packed full of fibre and contain no refined sweeteners.

150 g (5 oz) mixed-grain cereal
450 ml (16 fl oz) boiling water
175 g (6 oz) plain flour
1 tbsp baking powder

4 tbsp honey
Pinch of salt
1 lightly beaten egg
90 ml (3¼ fl oz) safflower oil

In a medium bowl, mix the cereal and water. Set aside for 20 minutes for the grains to swell.

Preheat the oven to 200°C (400°F / Gas mark 6). Grease a 12-cup muffin tin. In a medium bowl sieve the flour and baking powder.

In a large bowl, beat the honey, salt, egg and oil. Slowly add the flour and the cereal and mix well. Spoon the mixture into the prepared tin.

Bake in the oven for 20 minutes. Remove tin from the oven and cool for 5 minutes. Then remove the muffins and cool on a rack.

Store in an airtight container for up to 3 days, or freeze for up to 3 months.

Makes 1 dozen

dairy-free berry cupcakes

see variations page 352

These little treats are wonderful for the lactose-intolerant cupcake lover.

for the cupcakes
375 g (13 oz) mixed fresh berries (blueberries,
    strawberries, cranberries, blackberries)
225 g (8 oz) plain flour
115 g (4 oz) brown sugar
1 tbsp baking powder

4 tbsp vegetable oil
2 lightly beaten eggs

for the topping
125 g (4½ oz) mixed fruit jam

Preheat the oven to 175°C (350°F / Gas mark 4). Place 12 paper baking cases into a muffin tin. In a food processor, purée 240 g (8½ oz) of the berries until smooth.

In a small bowl, lightly crush the reserved berries with a fork. In a medium bowl, mix the flour, sugar and baking powder. In a large bowl, beat the oil and eggs. Add the puréed berries and mix well. Stir in the flour mixture until combined. Fold in the crushed berries. Spoon the batter into the cases. Top each cupcake with a teaspoon of jam. Bake for 20 minutes.

Remove tin from the oven and cool for 5 minutes. Remove the cupcakes and cool on a rack.

Store in an airtight container for up to 3 days, or freeze for up to 3 months.

Makes 1 dozen

gluten-free macadamia nut & raisin muffins

see variations page 353

Serve these to friends or kids as a treat and they will never know how healthy they are!

115 g (4 oz) soya bran
150 g (5 oz) finely ground, roasted
    macadamia nuts
190 g (6½ oz) brown sugar
1 tbsp baking powder
2 lightly beaten eggs

4 tbsp vegetable oil
4 tbsp butter, melted and cooled
175 ml (6 fl oz) milk
100 g (3½ oz) raisins
4 tbsp roughly chopped macadamia nuts

Preheat the oven to 190°C (375°F / Gas mark 5). Grease a 12-cup muffin tin.

In a medium bowl, mix the bran, nuts, sugar and baking powder. In a large bowl, beat the eggs, oil, butter and milk. Add the flour, mixing until nearly combined. Fold in the raisins and macadamia nuts.

Spoon the mixture into the prepared tin. Bake for about 20 minutes. Remove tin from the oven and cool for 5 minutes. Then remove the muffins and cool on a rack.

Store in an airtight container for up to 3 days, or freeze for up to 3 months.

Makes 1 dozen

gluten-free pecan cupcakes

see variations page 354

Gluten-free flour has a variety of uses. Look for it in speciality food or health shops. Add a little more liquid than you would when using normal flour, as it will be absorbed.

300 g (10½ oz) gluten-free plain flour
175 g (6 oz) caster sugar
1½ tbsp baking powder
Pinch of salt
2 lightly beaten eggs

4 tbsp unsalted butter, melted
300 ml (10½ fl oz) milk
1 tsp vanilla essence
150 g (5 oz) roughly chopped pecans
90 g (3¼ oz) chopped dates

Preheat the oven to 200°C (400°F / Gas mark 6). Grease a 12-cup muffin tin.

In a medium bowl, mix the flour, sugar, baking powder and salt. In a large bowl, beat the eggs, butter, milk and vanilla. Add the dry ingredients and stir until nearly combined. Fold in the pecans and dates.

Spoon the mixture into the prepared tin. Bake for 20 minutes. Remove tin from the oven and cool for 5 minutes. Then remove the muffins and cool on a rack.

Store in an airtight container for up to 3 days, or freeze for up to 3 months.

Makes 1 dozen

avocado & lemon muffins

see variations page 355

Avocados contain a host of essential oils, vitamins and minerals – all beneficial for the body's nervous system.

2 medium haas avocados, peeled and
    roughly chopped
1 tsp lemon juice
350 g (12 oz) plain flour
Pinch of salt
1 tbsp baking powder

2 lightly beaten eggs
225 ml (8 fl oz) milk
4 tbsp extra virgin olive oil
4 tbsp unsalted butter, melted
1½ tbsp lemon zest
1 tsp freshly ground black pepper

Preheat the oven to 200°C (400°F / Gas mark 6). Grease a 12-cup muffin tin. Place the avocado in a bowl with the lemon juice. Crush lightly with a fork.

In a medium bowl, mix the flour, salt and baking powder. Beat the remaining ingredients in a large bowl. Add the flour mixture, stirring until nearly combined. Fold in the avocado. Do not overmix.

Spoon the mixture into the prepared tin. Bake for 20 minutes. Remove tin from the oven and cool for 5 minutes. Then remove the muffins and cool on a rack.

Store in an airtight container for up to 2 days or freeze for up to 3 months.

Makes 1 dozen

variations

ultimate flourless choc cupcakes

see base recipe page 327

ultimate flourless peppermint cream cupcakes
Prepare the basic cupcake recipe. Substitute 1 teaspoon peppermint essence for the vanilla and orange essence.

ultimate flourless vanilla ice cream cupcakes
Prepare the basic cupcake recipe. Make an ice cream topping: mix 450 ml (16 fl oz) ready-made custard and 265 ml (9½ fl oz) whipping cream in a large bowl, and beat well. Add 1 teaspoon vanilla essence. Pour into an ice cream maker and churn until frozen. Put 1 scoop on top of each cupcake.

ultimate flourless strawberry cream cupcakes
Prepare the basic cupcake recipe. In the icing, substitute 1 teaspoon strawberry essence for the vanilla essence. Fold 100 g (3½ oz) finely chopped fresh strawberries after beating the cream.

variations

chocolate vegan cupcakes

see base recipe page 328

chocolate & orange vegan cupcakes
Prepare the basic cupcake recipe, adding 1½ tablespoons grated orange zest
to the mixture along with the chocolate chips.

chocolate & hazelnut vegan cupcakes
Prepare the basic cupcake recipe, adding 75 g (3 oz) chopped roasted
hazelnuts along with the chocolate chips.

chocolate & coffee vegan cupcakes
Prepare the basic cupcake recipe, adding 50 ml (2 fl oz) hot coffee to the
apple sauce mixture.

variations

g.i. carrot cupcakes

see base recipe page 331

g.i. pecan cupcakes
Prepare the basic cupcake mixture, substituting 115 g (4 oz) chopped pecans
for the walnuts.

g.i. banana cupcakes
Prepare the basic cupcake mixture, adding 125 g (4½ oz) mashed bananas
along with the carrots and fruits. Substitute ½ teaspoon nutmeg for
the mixed spice.

g.i. currant cupcakes
Prepare the basic cupcake mixture, substituting 200 g (7 oz) currants
for the raisins.

variations

egg-free chocolate cupcakes

see base recipe page 332

egg-free white chocolate cupcakes
Prepare the basic cupcake recipe, substituting 90 g (3¼ oz) white chocolate chips for the plain chocolate chips.

egg-free chocolate pecan cupcakes
Prepare the basic cupcake recipe, adding 90 g (3¼ oz) chopped pecans along with the chocolate chips.

egg-free chocolate macadamia cupcakes
Prepare the basic cupcake recipe, adding 90 g (3¼ oz) chopped macadamia nuts along with the chocolate chips.

variations

soy milk muffins

see base recipe page 335

soy milk & cranberry muffins
Prepare the basic muffin recipe, substituting 200 g (7 oz) dried cranberries for the raisins.

soy milk & apricot muffins
Prepare the basic muffin recipe, substituting 200 g (7 oz) chopped dried apricots for the raisins.

soy milk & blueberry muffins
Prepare the basic muffin recipe, substituting 200 g (7 oz) dried blueberries for the raisins.

sugar-free grain muffins

see base recipe page 336

sugar-free prune muffins
Prepare the basic muffin recipe, adding 4 tablespoons chopped dried prunes to the muffin batter.

sugar-free banana muffins
Prepare the basic muffin recipe, adding 125 g (4½ oz) mashed bananas to the muffin batter.

sugar-free pecan muffins
Prepare the basic muffin recipe, adding 115 g (4 oz) chopped pecans to the muffin batter.

variations

dairy-free berry cupcakes

see base recipe page 339

dairy-free apple & berry cupcakes
Prepare the basic muffin recipe, substituting 240 g (8½ oz) unsweetened apple sauce for 240 g (8½ oz) of the mixed berries.

dairy-free nectarine & berry cupcakes
Prepare the basic muffin recipe, substituting 240 g (8½ oz) puréed canned nectarines for 240 g (8½ oz) of the mixed berries.

dairy-free peach & berry cupcakes
Prepare the basic muffin recipe, substituting 240 g (8½ oz) puréed canned peaches for 240 g (8½ oz) of the mixed berries.

gluten-free macademia nut & raisin muffins

see base recipe page 340

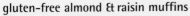

gluten-free almond & raisin muffins
Prepare the basic muffin recipe, substituting 150 g (5 oz) ground almonds for the ground macadamia nuts. Replace the 4 tablespoons chopped macadamia nuts with 4 tablespoons chopped blanched almonds.

gluten-free macademia nut & cranberry muffins
Prepare the basic muffin recipe, substituting 75 g (3 oz) dried cranberries for the sultanas.

gluten-free macademia nut & cherry muffins
Prepare the basic muffin recipe, substituting 75 g (3 oz) dried cherries for the sultanas.

variations

gluten-free pecan cupcakes

see base recipe page 343

gluten-free mixed peel cupcakes
Prepare the basic cupcake recipe, substituting 90 g (3¼ oz) chopped
crystallised mixed peel for the dates.

gluten-free apricot cupcakes
Prepare the basic cupcake recipe, substituting 90 g (3¼ oz) chopped dried
apricots for the dates.

gluten-free molasses cupcakes
Prepare the basic cupcake recipe, omitting the sugar and adding
4 tablespoons molasses and 4 tablespoons of honey to the milk mixture.

variations

avocado & lemon muffins

see base recipe page 344

chilli, avocado & lemon muffins
Prepare the basic muffin recipe, adding 1 tablespoon seeded and finely chopped chilli to the egg mixture.

avocado & orange muffins
Prepare the basic muffin recipe, substituting 1 tablespoon grated orange zest for the lemon zest.

avocado & tomato muffins
Prepare the basic muffin recipe, adding 3 tablespoons chopped sun-dried tomatoes to the batter after the flour has been added.

index